superseries

Managing Customer Service

FIFTH EDITION

Published for the
Institute of Leadership & Management

ELSEVIER

AMSTERDAM • BOSTON • HEIDELBERG • LONDON • NEW YORK • OXFORD
PARIS • SAN DIEGO • SAN FRANCISCO • SINGAPORE • SYDNEY • TOKYO
Pergamon Flexible Learning is an imprint of Elsevier

Pergamon
Flexible
Learning

Pergamon Flexible Learning is an imprint of Elsevier
Linacre House, Jordan Hill, Oxford OX2 8DP, UK
30 Corporate Drive, Suite 400, Burlington, MA 01803, USA

First edition 1986
Second edition 1991
Third edition 1997
Fourth edition 2003
Fifth edition 2007

Editor: David Pardey

Based on material in previous editions of this work

British Library Cataloguing in Publication Data
A catalogue record for this book is available from the British Library

Library of Congress Cataloguing in Publication Data
A catalogue record for this book is available from the Library of Congress

ISBN 978-0-08-046419-0

For information on all Pergamon Flexible Learning publications
visit our website at http://books.elsevier.com

Institute of Leadership & Management
Registered Office
1 Giltspur Street
London
EC1A 9DD
Telephone: 020 7294 2470
www.i-l-m.com
ILM is part of the City & Guilds Group

Typeset by Charon Tec Ltd (A Macmillan Company), Chennai, India
www.charontec.com
Printed and bound in Great Britain

07 08 09 10 11   10 9 8 7 6 5 4 3 2 1

Contents

Series preface	v
Unit specification	vii

Workbook introduction   ix

1	ILM Super Series study links	ix
2	Links to ILM qualifications	ix
3	Links to S/NVQs in management	ix
4	Workbook objectives	x
5	Activity planner	xi

Session A   About customers   1

1	Introduction	1
2	What is a customer?	1
3	Non-commercial organizations and their customers	3
4	External customers	6
5	Internal customers	8
6	Summary	15

Session B   What is customer care?   17

1	Introduction	17
2	Customers old and new	17
3	The three pillars of customer satisfaction	23
4	Meeting the needs of external customers	28
5	The quality of personal service	36
6	Telephone contacts	42
7	Summary	49

Contents

Session C   Delivering customer care   51

    1   Introduction   51
    2   Identifying your customer care problems   51
    3   Managing for customer satisfaction   67
    4   Setting and monitoring standards   72
    5   A customer care culture?   77
    6   Summary   81

Performance checks   83

    1   Quick quiz   83
    2   Workbook assessment   85
    3   Work-based assignment   86

Reflect and review   89

    1   Reflect and review   89
    2   Action plan   92
    3   Extensions   94
    4   Answers to self-assessment questions   95
    5   Answers to activities   98
    6   Answers to the quick quiz   98
    7   Certificate   99

Series preface

Whether you are a tutor/trainer or studying management development to further your career, Super Series provides an exciting and flexible resource to help you to achieve your goals. The fifth edition is completely new and up-to-date, and has been structured to perfectly match the Institute of Leadership & Management (ILM)'s new unit-based qualifications for first line managers. It also harmonizes with the 2004 national occupational standards in management and leadership, providing an invaluable resource for S/NVQs at Level 3 in Management.

Super Series is equally valuable for anyone tutoring or studying any management programmes at this level, whether leading to a qualification or not. Individual workbooks also support short programmes, which may be recognized by ILM as Endorsed or Development Awards, or provide the ideal way to undertake CPD activities.

For learners, coping with all the pressures of today's world, Super Series offers you the flexibility to study at your own pace to fit around your professional and other commitments. You don't need a PC or to attend classes at a specific time – choose when and where to study to suit yourself! And you will always have the complete workbook as a quick reference just when you need it.

For tutors/trainers, Super Series provides an invaluable guide to what needs to be covered, and in what depth. It also allows learners who miss occasional sessions to 'catch up' by dipping into the series.

Super Series provides unrivalled support for all those involved in first line management and supervision.

Unit specification

Title:	Managing customer service		Unit Ref:	M3.08
Level:	3			
Credit value:	2			

Learning outcomes	Assessment criteria	
The learner will	The learner can (in an organization with which the learner is familiar)	
1. Understand marketing	3.1	Explain the marketing concept and why it is relevant for managers
	3.2	Conduct a simple organizational SWOT analysis in the marketing context
	3.3	Describe the *four* elements of the marketing mix and give an example of how each is used within the context of the organization
2. Understand customer service	2.1	Briefly describe at least two legal rights of customers
	2.2	Briefly describe *two* of the organization's commitments to customers
	2.3	Briefly describe the manager's responsibilities in relation to customer service
3. Understand caring for the customer	1.1	Identify an external and an internal customer of the organization
	1.2	Describe how customer needs are identified
	1.3	Explain how customer service standards and procedures are used to meet customer needs
	1.4	Explain how you could monitor customer service against the standards set

Workbook introduction

1 ILM Super Series study links

This workbook addresses the issues of *Managing Customer Service*. Should you wish to extend your study to other Super Series workbooks covering related or different subject areas, you will find a comprehensive list at the back of this book.

2 Links to ILM qualifications

This workbook relates to the learning outcomes of Unit M3.08 Managing customer service from the ILM Level 3 Award, Certificate and Diploma in First Line Management.

3 Links to S/NVQs in management

This workbook relates to the following Unit of the Management Standards which are used in S/NVQs in Management, as well as a range of other S/NVQs:

F5. Resolve customer service problems

4 Workbook objectives

It is a highly competitive world, and every organization is under increasing pressure to offer its customers a better deal. Trouble lies in store for those that fail to do so.

Customer care is often thought of as the up-front niceties offered to the customer at the point of sale or delivery, but this is far from being the whole story. The modern-day aim of total customer satisfaction can only be achieved when every aspect of the organization's activities, from product design to customer information, and every single person, from the chief executive to the most junior employee, is geared and committed to meeting the customer's needs.

All of this ultimately depends on people, and the performance of people depends on the quality of management. Their job is to achieve a difficult but crucial balance. They must keep customers happy, but they must also ensure that the organization meets its financial targets. It's easy for this to go out of balance.

In this workbook we will look at what is meant by the terms *external customer* and *internal customer* and explore the reasons why we are all so dependent on our customers. In doing so, we will examine the factors that contribute to customer satisfaction and consider what sort of service customers expect. We will then go on to look at some practical steps that you can take to improve the quality of customer care provided by your team and organization.

4.1 Objectives

When you have completed this workbook you will be better able to:

- explain the meaning and significance of customer care;
- identify your internal and external customers;
- identify your customers' needs and any areas in which you are failing to meet them;
- provide an effective lead for your team in raising the standard of customer care;
- ensure that you and your team members perform to a high standard in customer-contact situations.

5 Activity planner

The following Activities require some planning so you may want to look at these now.

Activity 4 asks you to discuss the core business, customers and customer needs with your colleagues.

Activity 8 suggests that you may find it helpful to discuss the needs of your internal customers with the customers themselves.

Activity 29 asks you to review with your team the level of customer service you provide.

Activity 37 invites you to survey your customer's perception of the care you provide by questionnaire or telephone interview. You may want to involve your work team in this.

Some or all of the Activities may provide the basis of evidence for your S/NVQ portfolio. All Portfolio Activities and the Work-based assignment are signposted with this icon.

The icon states the elements to which the Portfolio Activities and Work-based assignment relate.

Session A
About customers

1 Introduction

Before you decide how to care for your customers, you need to establish who they are. This may not be as obvious as it seems. *A customer is not just someone who buys something from you; both commercial and non-commercial organizations have customers.*

The message of this session will be that:

■ every organization needs to identify its external customers;
■ every organization should ensure that it is in the business of meeting customer needs.

In addition, everyone working inside an organization also has internal customers, whose needs also have to be met.

2 What is a customer?

We have established that there are more of them than you might at first think. But who are they exactly?

Activity 1

2 mins

Try to say in a sentence or two what you think is meant by a customer.

_____

_____

_____

_____

_____

A manager of a menswear shop would probably say that customers are the individuals who come into the shop to look at the goods, and perhaps to buy.

Someone working in the sales team of a manufacturing company probably thinks of customers as:

> In the commercial sector, a customer is someone who buys our goods and services.

- the organizations that buy from the company; and
- the individuals within them who make the purchasing decisions.

It is obvious that all of the following organizations have customers (though the solicitors and architects probably call them clients):

retailers	restaurants and hotels
travel agents	firms of solicitors
manufacturing firms	car rental companies
architects	building societies
wholesalers	insurance companies
bus companies	haulage firms

Anyone who works at the sharp end of a commercial organization knows that customers are **extremely important**. Let's analyse why exactly this is.

If customers don't like what a firm has to offer, they can simply choose another. If enough customers do this, they have the power to damage and even destroy the organizations whose offer they reject. This is the market at work.

> Customers not only have **choice**: they also have **power** – spending power. That's why so many organizations say **the most important person in our business is the customer.**

Organizations that live by supplying goods and services to the market have **no choice** but to **compete** for customers: their survival depends on it. They also have to listen carefully to the messages that customers send them when they make their choices.

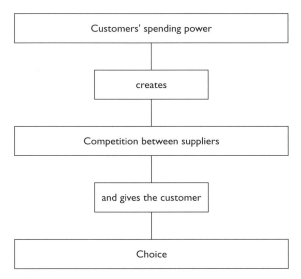

The Market at work

Whenever you buy something from one supplier you are sending a message to any competing suppliers that you know of. That message is that something about their offer is wrong, and that they are going to have to try harder next time.

We can sum up the situation in the commercial sector by saying:

■ with few exceptions, many suppliers compete for any profitable market;
■ customers have plenty of choice;
■ suppliers who fail to provide what their customers need are asking for trouble.

3 Non-commercial organizations and their customers

But what about non-commercial organizations? Don't they operate in a different way? Do they even have customers?

Activity 2

Which of the following organizations would you say have 'customers'? Tick those that in your opinion do.

Boots stores	❏
The Central Library	❏
Your local NHS Hospital	❏
Glosser & Slant (Public Relations Consultants)	❏
BT	❏
The Railway Hotel	❏
The local Further Education College	❏
British Gas	❏
The Probation Service	❏

There is no argument about the commercial organizations in the list: obviously they must have customers, because they are dependent on selling goods or services in the market. But what about the non-commercial organizations in the list?

- The Central Library serves people who want to borrow books.
- The County NHS Hospital serves people who are ill.
- The Further Education College serves its students, and to some extent their parents and future employers.
- The Probation Service serves the Courts, the community, and people who are in trouble with the law.

These are publicly funded organizations whose services are mostly **free**. They do not have **paying customers**. Traditionally, they did not think of the people who use their services as 'customers' at all.

However, since the 1990s this attitude has changed greatly. Let's take the NHS as an example.

Activity 3 ·

5 mins

Think about the way a hospital operates. What difference do you think it makes when a hospital regards the people it serves not only as patients but also as customers?

_____

_____

_____

_____

In the past the attitude was that:

■ hospitals are a free service for which patients ought to be grateful;
■ patients should be expected to fit in with the routines that suit the hospital and its staff.

Hospitals focused on the basic need of patients to have their health problem dealt with and took little account of patients' other needs. As a result:

■ doctors seldom bothered to explain anything to the patients;
■ visiting hours were very restricted;
■ the whole atmosphere was severe and forbidding;
■ the facilities were minimal and the décor depressing.

Today there is a trend towards taking account of other needs, which include those for:

■ hotel services, such as a friendly reception, a good night's sleep, comfort, lounges in which to read or watch TV, access to telephones etc.;
■ proper information and advice for patients about their condition;
■ more information about the range of treatments available, including counselling for people with serious or incurable conditions;
■ the widest possible access for family and friends;
■ a choice of good-quality meals.

A visit to hospital used to be a rather intimidating experience, but now that hospitals have become more customer-friendly, a great deal has changed. Fewer doctors talk down to their patients; reception areas are warmer and more comfortable, with shops, cafés and children's playrooms. And visiting hours have become much more flexible.

The trend towards considering users of a non-commercial service as customers whose needs must be met has become far more widely accepted across most of the public sector.

4 External customers

So far we have been considering the relationship between an organization and its external customers. These may be actual customers or potential customers – that is, people or organizations who may become customers in the future. So who exactly are your organization's external customers? The answer may not be as simple as you first think.

Most organizations have different groups of customers, all with different needs or wants. For some, particularly in manufacturing, this is not a problem. They can simply produce different products for different groups, as in the case of a car manufacturer that produces a range of models from comparatively cheap to expensive. It can be more complicated for service industries. What, for example, should a hotel do whose present customers include both young people who want a lively bar with music, and older people who want peace and quiet? Should it forget about the needs of one group and so put off potential customers from that group or 'segment' of the population?

In answering a question like this, the hotel must consider what business it is in – or wants to be in. Is it in the business of meeting the needs of young people for a place to stay that provides some good night-life, or is it in the business of catering for people who want comfort and quiet relaxation? Only once this question has been answered can it begin to consider what the exact needs of its customers, both actual and potential, are.

Activity 4

S/NVQ F6

This Activity may provide the basis of appropriate evidence for your S/NVQ portfolio. If you are intending to take this course of action, it might be better to write your answers on separate sheets of paper.

You may need to talk to other people in your organization in order to answer some of the following questions.

1   What business is your organization in?

_____

_____

2   Who are your organization's existing external customers? (Remember, you may need to think of them as a number of different segments.)

_____

_____

_____

3   What are these customers' needs?

_____

_____

_____

4   Are these needs being met? If not, or not adequately, why not?

_____

_____

_____

5   Are there any groups or segments whom your organization regards as potential customers?

_____

_____

_____

6   Are the needs of these potential customers different from those of existing customers? If so, in what way are they different?

_____

_____

_____

7 Can these needs be met while continuing to meet the needs of existing customers? If so, how?

_____

_____

_____

8 What steps should be taken to improve the organization's approach to customers?

_____

_____

_____

9 What contribution could you yourself make towards achieving this (i.e. by changing the way you and your team operate)?

_____

_____

_____

Whatever kind of organization you work for, it should be in the business of meeting its customers' needs; and you should take a broad view of these. Customers' needs go beyond the basic goods and services which you provide. If you identified shortcomings in the approach to customers (and no organization is perfect) you should try to ensure that something is done about them. At a minimum you should make sure that your own team has the right attitude and performs in the right way.

5 Internal customers

As a manager you not only have the needs of external customers to think about, you also have those of your internal customers to consider. Your internal customers are the people within your organization who receive things from you. Take a restaurant as an example. An external customer sits down at a table and gives an order to one of the waitresses. The waitress then hands over the order to the chef, who then asks a kitchen assistant to prepare certain ingredients. He may also ask the dishwasher to hand over some clean plates or dishes on which he can arrange the cooked food. In this scenario, the chef is the internal customer of the kitchen assistant and the dishwasher, while the waitress is the internal customer of the chef.

Now let's turn to another, more complicated example, that of a large hospital.

Large hospitals exist to serve external customers (patients, their families, the Health Authorities, etc.). Their main burden of service is carried by their front-line departments:

- medical;
- obstetrics and gynaecology;
- surgical;
- genito-urinary;
- psychiatric;
- geriatric, etc.

However, there are also various internal service departments whose job is to support the work of the front-line departments. Catering is an obvious example.

Activity 5

3 mins

What other internal services would you expect to find in a large general hospital? Try to list at least **six:**

_____

_____

_____

You probably listed at least some of these:

■ boiler room;	■ nursing;	■ physiotherapy;
■ counselling;	■ nurse training;	■ reception;
■ cleaning;	■ pathology lab;	■ security;
■ maintenance;	■ pharmacy;	■ X-ray.

> Internal customers may not be paying you, but if you fail to meet their needs, the people who hold the purse strings will soon get to know.

Some of these departments – like reception, nursing and counselling – obviously have a front-line customer-contact role too, but their main purpose is to contribute to the work of the treatment departments.

The diagram below shows how we can map out this network of service relationships.

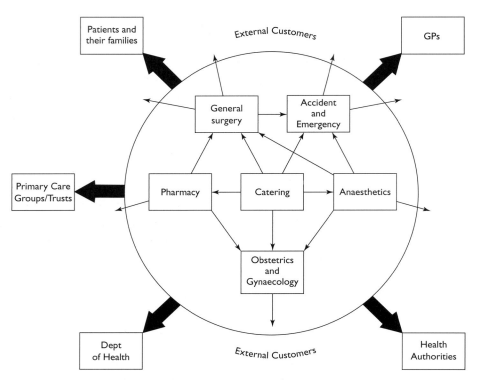

Network of service relationships in a hospital

The real picture is even more complex, because there are many departments that we have not shown, including those concerned with management. However, this figure clearly shows that there are plenty of internal, as well as external, customers here.

Activity 6

2 mins

Who would you say the X-ray Department's customers are?

_____

_____

_____

_____

The Department serves both external customers:

■ the patients that other departments send to be X-rayed;

and internal customers:

■ the front-line medical and surgical departments that send the patients and need to see their X-rays (medical and surgical departments);
■ the hospital management, which is responsible for ensuring that the hospital as a whole functions properly in the interests of its patients.

The hospital consists of a complex network of customer–supplier relationships in which:

■ the hospital as a whole serves its external customers;
■ the front-line departments carry the main burden of customer service;
■ the second-line departments help them to carry the burden of customer service.

Commercial organizations have a network of internal customers too.

Organizations are like complicated machines:

■ all the different parts are connected;
■ even the smallest parts play a role in making the machine work.

When one department isn't pulling its weight, it is like a bike with a missing pedal, or a car missing on one cylinder. In the race for competitive success, it will soon start falling behind, as this case study shows.

> Benedorma was a Europe-wide hotel chain, catering for business travellers. It operated a central reservations system, based in Paris. Any customer could call Paris free of charge and book a room in any Benedorma hotel.
>
> The staff in the reservations service were efficient and pleasant; so for the most part were the staff in the various hotels.
>
> Benedorma accepted reservations at very short notice, but customers who booked less than 24 hours ahead often found that there was no room for them when they arrived. This was because the hotel had not been notified of the reservation.
>
> There were numerous complaints from customers, and hotel managers became very critical of the reservations system.
>
> An inquiry found that the fault lay with the despatching department which was responsible for passing reservations on to the hotels.

The despatchers responded by saying that Benedorma did not offer an absolute guarantee of a room for someone booking within 24 hours of occupancy (which was technically true). Despatching staff worked a normal day shift and stopped work at 6.00 pm. If they were particularly busy, some reservations would be left over until the next day, and it was the short-notice bookings among these which caused the problem.

Benedorma's answer to this customer care problem was:

1 to change its policy so that every accepted booking carried a guarantee that the room would be ready and waiting;

2 to retrain the despatching staff;

3 to change the despatching procedures so that short-notice reservations would be separated out for priority handling.

Finally, let's consider your own position.

Activity 7   5 mins

Think carefully about your own situation at work. Even if you work in a front-line customer contact role, you will also have your own internal customers. Who are they?

_____

_____

_____

_____

_____

_____

Exactly who your internal customers are will, of course, depend on your particular situation. But they will almost certainly include:

■ your immediate manager, to whom you report formally;

- the people who report to you and require a variety of things from you, including information, instructions, guidance, coaching and appraisal;
- people outside your own department who require you (and your staff) to provide them with raw materials, semi-finished or finished goods, tools or conditions (such as the correct temperature or lighting); or services such as information, instructions, training and ideas.

Activity 8

S/NVQ F6

This Activity may provide the basis of appropriate evidence for your S/NVQ portfolio. If you are intending to take this course of action, it might be better to write your answers on separate sheets of paper.

1 Go back to the list of internal customers you drew up in Activity 7. What needs do each of these internal customers have in relation to you? (You may find it helpful to discuss this question with the internal customers themselves.)

_____

_____

_____

2 What do you do to meet these needs?

_____

_____

_____

3 In what ways might you better meet these needs?

_____

_____

_____

In every line of work, serving the external customers is the top priority.

And if you're not serving those customers, you'd better be serving someone who is!

Self-assessment 1

12 mins

1   Fill in the blanks in these sentences so that they make sense:

Our _____ customers are the people outside the organization to whom we supply a service or product. They may be actual or _____ customers. Our _____ customers are the people within the organization to whom we supply something.

2   Explain briefly why it would be useful to regard your own manager as a customer.

_____

_____

_____

_____

3   Draw up a diagram showing the internal and external relationships which exist in a prison. You may want to draft this out on scrap paper before putting your considered version below. Include the following:

The Home Office;
The Courts;
The local community;
Prisoners;
Prisoners' families;
Prison Officers;
The Governor's office;
The administration office;
The catering service.

Answers to these questions can be found on pages 130–1.

6 Summary

■ Both commercial and non-commercial organizations have customers.

■ Customers are the people whom we serve, whether they pay for our services or not.

■ Commercial organizations need to provide good service because they depend directly on competing for their customers' spending power.

■ Non-commercial organizations also stand to benefit from providing good service – more efficiency, more job-satisfaction, more job security.

■ Everyone has customers:

  ■ organizations have external customers, both actual and potential;
  ■ departments and individuals have internal customers as well.

■ If internal suppliers aren't serving their internal customers properly, the external customers won't be served properly either.

■ Not everyone is in the front line of customer service – but if you aren't serving customers yourself, you should be serving someone who is.

Session B
What is customer care?

1 Introduction

Customer care is often misunderstood. People tend to assume that:

- it is all about being courteous and friendly to customers;
- only customer-contact staff need to bother about it.

This is quite wrong: customer contact is an important area (which we will look at in Session C), but seeing polite smiles is not the customer's top priority.

Customer care is in effect part of marketing, and it plays a crucial part in ensuring the success of any organization. Unless it covers every aspect of the service provided to customers, ensuring that their needs and wants are met, it will not work.

2 Customers old and new

Customer care can be defined as:

'serving the customer in a way that meets their needs and wants'

This is not the same as winning new customers, though many commercial firms devote a great deal of time and energy to doing this, through their sales and marketing activities.

> McGibbons is a pharmaceutical company which makes and sells drugs used for treating severe asthma. Its primary customers are family doctors and hospital specialists, because these have the authority to prescribe drugs, and can opt for McGibbons' drugs rather than those of a competitor.
>
> Out of McGibbons' 520 staff, 100 are employed in some aspect of sales or marketing.
>
> The Marketing Department itself consists of 20 people. They are responsible for working out strategy and controlling the annual advertising and promotion spend of £6,000,000.
>
> The Sales Department includes 40 sales representatives who spend most of their time on the road visiting the primary customers.
>
> The remaining 40 sales and marketing staff are involved in various sales support activities.

Activity 9 ·   3 mins

From what you know of representatives and selling, what would you say the main tasks of McGibbons' representatives would be?

_____

_____

_____

If they are like most sales representatives, they will have three main tasks on their agenda:

- identifying potential new customers and trying to win them;
- keeping existing customers happy;
- trying to sell new products to existing customers.

Anyone in this line of work will tell you that the first of these is extremely difficult. It is also expensive.

> It costs McGibbons £35,000 a year to keep a representative and his or her car on the road. They reckon that each representative spends about a quarter of his or her time trying to win new customers, and that the average number of new customers won per representative per year is 20. This is a cost of £35,000 ÷ 4 ÷ 20 = £437.50. (The true cost per net new customer is higher, because each representative also loses a few customers for various reasons.)
>
> McGibbons also considers that £1.6 million of the advertising and promotion budget should be allocated to the winning of new customers. £1.6 million ÷ 20 ÷ 40 (the number of representatives) = £2,000. So the total cost per new customer won is a staggering £2,437.50!

In many industries like insurance, banking and retailing a new customer costs less than this, but there are also sectors like defence, construction, avionics and heavy engineering where the customers are few but their purchasing power huge. In these sectors, the cost of winning a new customer can be colossal.

Activity 10 ·

5 mins

Salespeople are in constant direct contact with their customers. Suppose you are such a customer, responsible for purchasing building materials for a local council's building maintenance department, for example. You will have a number of regular suppliers, and you will deal with their representatives.

What would these representatives need to do to keep you, as the customer, happy? (If you don't work in this kind of role, why not consult a colleague who does, before you answer?)

_____

_____

_____

_____

_____

Most people in this position prefer to deal with representatives who:

- know their products thoroughly and can give reliable advice;
- are pleasant to deal with (friendly, but not over-friendly);
- are efficient (business-like but not pushy);
- are honest and truthful;
- listen to customers and act on their wishes;
- give the impression that customers are their top priority.

'Customer care is not:

- flavour of the month.
- a campaign which runs for six months and then stops.
- "smile training" or "charm school ethics".
- placing posters around the premises with such slogans as "the customer is king" ...
- something just for front-line staff.
- something that will bring instant results.
- a belief that "the customer is always right".
- something that starts after a sale is made.'

Andrew Brown (1989), *Customer Care Management*

And every successful representative knows that keeping an existing customer is:

ten times easier

and

ten times cheaper

than winning a new customer to replace one you have lost.

Unfortunately, many organizations have not yet discovered this important truth. They wrongly believe that:

- customer care is about slick salespeople, sweet smiles and saying 'have a nice day';
- customer care is solely the concern of the customer-contact staff.

Certainly, skilful sales staff and good manners help, but on their own they are not enough, as this case study shows.

On moving into his new house, Amal had a new combination boiler and central heating system installed by Dozey Heating, and then took out a service agreement with the company. For a few years there was no problem and the technicians who came on an annual basis to service the system had very little to do. However, Amal then noticed that the boiler was making a loud noise whenever it fired up. Furthermore, the problem seemed to be related to a constant fall in pressure. In fact, Amal was beginning to find it necessary to adjust the pressure every day rather than two or three times a year as normal.

The technician sent by Dozey Heating to look at the problem announced that it would be solved by descaling the boiler, but this was a remedy not covered by the service agreement so there would be an additional charge of £190. A second technician arrived to carry out the descaling, but after he departed Amal found that the boiler was as noisy as ever and the pressure was still falling to zero. He rung Dozey Heating's Service Department. They were very apologetic, but said it would be another three days before a third technician could call round. When he eventually arrived, this technician was very friendly but told Amal that the descaling had not been the right solution and what was far more likely to be causing the problem was a leaking radiator. Unfortunately, to discover where the leak was, Amal would have to pull up all the floorboards.

Amal spent the night worrying about it all and rang up Dozey Heating the next morning to express his concern and his dissatisfaction with the service he had received so far. The woman he spoke to, who was in the Customer Relations Department, was very sympathetic and made an appointment for their most senior technician to call round. However, the next day Amal received an invoice from Dozey for the descaling job. Thinking that the invoice must have been sent out before his phone call, he decided to ignore it. The senior technician arrived the next day, was extremely apologetic about all that had happened, and diagnosed the cause of the problem as a faulty valve. The valve was replaced under Amal's service agreement, the boiler stopped making a noise and losing pressure – and Amal went on holiday thinking that the whole sorry saga was over at last. But on his return there was a letter waiting for him which said that if he did not pay for the descaling job within seven days, court proceedings would be initiated. He could not believe his eyes. He wrote a long letter to the Customer Relations Department outlining exactly what had happened and why he was justified in not paying. The next day he received a phone call from the head of Customer Relations, who apologized profusely and agreed that the invoice should never have been sent in the first place. It was, she said, all down to a computer error. But it was too late as far as Amal was concerned. He wanted nothing more to do with the company.

Activity 11

6 mins

The people working for Dozey Heating did some things that were right, and others that were wrong. Read through the case study again carefully, and list all the points you can identify.

Done right:

_____

_____

_____

Done wrong:

_____

_____

_____

_____

_____

Dozey's staff were pleasant and apologetic at the right times, and the head of Customer Relations responded very promptly to Amal's final letter.

On the other hand, the service they actually delivered was very poor:

■ two technicians failed to diagnose the problem correctly, and one of them caused a great deal of stress for Amal;

■ there were too many delays between visits by the various technicians;

■ there was an obvious lack of communication between the Customer Relations and Accounts Departments.

When this sort of thing happens, there is a tendency to blame 'the system' or 'the computer', but the responsibility actually lies with the human beings in charge of the various stages of the system. The sales and marketing people won a customer. The Service, Customer Relations and Accounts people lost him.

Activity 12

4 mins

This episode was bad news for Dozey Heating in **three** important respects. Think about the situation, and see if you can define what they are:

1 _____

2 _____

3 _____

First, they lost a customer, lost turnover and lost profit. Second, the episode took up a large amount of staff time (and time is money). Third, their reputation was damaged.

> A damaged reputation is no joke. Research has shown that:
>
> ■ a **satisfied customer** tends to tell about four other people;
> ■ a **dissatisfied** one tends to tell an average of sixteen.

It is very easy to get a bad reputation for service, and very hard to get a good one.

3 The three pillars of customer satisfaction

It is the task of every organization to provide its customers with:

■ the right product;
■ at the right place;
■ at the right time;
■ at the right price (in the case of public services that are free at the point of use, this is the amount that taxpayers have to contribute to keep the service going);
■ in the right way.

The Dozey Heating case study shows that the personal niceties side of customer care is far from being the crucial factor in satisfying — and therefore keeping — customers. Customer care is about getting the package we offer the customer right **as a whole.**

So what are the other factors involved? Let's start by considering an ordinary consumer.

> Neville wants a new front door for his house, and within half an hour's drive of where he lives there are eight firms where he can buy one.
>
> There is plenty of choice, and Neville has been a customer of all eight at some time or other. How does he decide which to go to this time? His decision will probably be based on weighing up a number of factors.

Activity 13 · 4 mins

There are many factors which might influence Neville's decision. List as many as you can think of:

_____

_____

_____

_____

_____

_____

You have almost certainly had experience of this kind of shopping and so will agree with this list of the main questions that Neville might ask himself.

- Do they stock the style of door I want?
- Have they got a reasonable selection in stock?
- How competitive is the price?
- How good is the quality?
- How near is the store?
- How crowded will it be?
- How close can I park?
- Will they be open at the time I want to go?

- Do they take credit cards?
- Do the staff know their stuff?
- Are they pleasant and helpful?
- If there turns out to be a problem with the door after I have bought it, what will their attitude be?

Activity 14

6 mins

All these 'satisfaction factors' can be grouped under one of the **three** headings below. Try doing so yourself.

Product factors (the right product at the right price)

_____

_____

_____

_____

Convenience factors (at the right place at the right time)

_____

_____

_____

_____

Human factors (in the right way)

_____

_____

_____

_____

The diagram below shows a way of grouping these three pillars of customer satisfaction.

Customer satisfaction		
Product factors • the range on offer; • the price; • the quality and specification; • the standard of 'aftercare', etc.	**Convenience factors** • location; • parking facilities; • opening times, etc.; • payment arrangements.	**Human factors** • speed of service; • skill and knowledge of staff; • attitude and behaviour of staff.

Customer satisfaction: the three pillars

Activity 15

2 mins

Which of these three pillars of customer satisfaction is the most important?

■ the product factors;
■ the convenience factors; or
■ the human factors?

Explain briefly why you think so:

_____

_____

_____

'Customer care has to have its roots in a company's culture and corporate beliefs. It cannot be grafted on to a business as an afterthought.'

Andrew Brown (1989), *Customer Care Management*

It depends to some extent on the situation. For example:

■ if the product and the price are not right, it scarcely matters whether the staff are nice or nasty;
■ if the price is a real bargain, customers may put up with a lot of inconvenience;
■ if the product is widely available at the same price everywhere, the human factor may be very important indeed.

But what both private and commercial customers need above all from the goods or services supplied to them is:

complete reliability

and

no surprises.

This means that in a customer care programme the product factors usually come first and the human factors last. All the friendly smiles and polite greetings in the world will not compensate for unreliable goods or substandard services.

Now let's consider a commercial situation and see what satisfaction factors apply there.

Activity 16

4 mins

Tom is a team leader with a major DIY retailer. He deals with two suppliers of doors – Woodhull Ltd and Claflin Ltd. They both provide the same product specification, price and quality, so product factors are not an issue.

Which other satisfaction factors do you think Tom, as a customer of these two firms, would judge them on?

Convenience factors:

_____

_____

_____

_____

Human factors:

_____

_____

_____

_____

The key issues would probably be:

■ Convenience factors: the flexibility of the service.

 – Can they change delivery schedules if need be?
 – Can they deliver unscheduled requirements at short notice if need be?
 – Are they willing to take back surplus stocks?

■ Human factors: the efficiency of the staff.

 – Do they act promptly?
 – Do they pass on messages?
 – Do they get things right?
 – Do deliveries arrive when promised?
 – Do they match the order properly?

■ Human factors: the personal qualities of the staff.

 – Are they friendly?
 – Are they helpful?
 – Do they make an effort to get things right?

The product factors meet Tom's stated needs and it is essential that they are right. But this doesn't mean that the convenience and human factors are not important. They, in fact, meet Tom's unstated needs or wants. In other words, they are the things that will particularly please Tom, and the supplier who gets them right is more likely to win Tom's custom.

4 Meeting the needs of external customers

In general, external customers have a need for a service that is reasonably efficient, flexible and helpful, considering the circumstances, the price being paid, and the state of the trade.

Activity 17

10 mins

If you do not work in a direct customer-contact role, you may need to consult colleagues who do in order to complete this Activity.

1   Write down the main product (goods or services) that your organization supplies (choose just one of them if there are several):

_____

2   Who are your main competitors in supplying this product?

_____

_____

3   Comparing your organization with its competitors, in what ways do you think it does better in meeting customer needs? (Think about product, convenience and human factors.)

_____

_____

_____

4   In what ways do you think your organization does worse?

_____

_____

_____

Perhaps you found it difficult to answer these questions. Indeed:

■   perhaps your organization has no competitors, because it has a monopoly, or because you work in a public service that is not subject to direct competition;
■   perhaps there is nothing to choose between your organization and its various competitors.

> Customers don't necessarily tell you when they are dissatisfied. They just take their business elsewhere.

However, if at all possible, you as a manager must answer these questions in considering how to improve the contribution that you and your team make to meeting customer needs. This applies whether or not you have direct contact with external customers, as the following example shows.

Activity 18

4 mins

Indu works for an educational charity that gives study grants to people who can't get them through their local authority. Her job is to process new applications for grants. When she has finished with each application she sends it on to another department. She has occasionally spoken to an external customer (a grant applicant) on the phone, but has never met one face to face.

The charity wants to improve the standard of customer care in relation to its external customers (people who apply for grants). What significance do you think this has for Indu?

_____

_____

_____

_____

The charity as a whole has many external customers, and some staff have a lot of direct contact with them. Indu's position is different but she does play an important part in caring for the customer by ensuring that she:

■ processes applications speedily and accurately;
■ notes any points which might need to be queried with the applicant.

Customers expect an efficient and reliable service, and simply by doing her job **conscientiously** Indu can improve the standard of customer care.

This applies equally to Indu's internal customers:

■ the department to which she sends the processed applications;
■ management;
■ colleagues in her own section who rely on her pulling her weight.

Activity 19

How can you tell whether your organization is meeting its customers' needs? (Again, you may need to consult colleagues about this.)

_____

_____

_____

The best organizations are keenly interested in what their customers think of them. If your own organization is one of these it will:

- keep a careful log of complaints;
- listen carefully to reports from the customer-contact staff;
- measure and carefully study the level of sales, inquiries, customer throughput and other indicators of performance.

If complaints are increasing, sales are falling and the customer-contact staff are increasingly harassed, then this strongly suggests that customers' needs are not being met.

It is important to **listen for dissatisfaction**, and the earlier this is done, the better. This means:

- finding out what customers' needs are;
- finding out how well the organization is meeting these needs;
- taking action to bridge the 'needs gap'.

4.1 Market research

Finding out what customers' needs are may require some market research. This is generally carried out by specialists and takes two basic forms:

- desk or secondary research;
- field or primary research.

Desk research involves finding out all the relevant facts that have already been written about the market for a product and the needs of customers within that market. Secondary data often provides a starting point for research and is comparatively cheap and easy to access. Nowadays, sources include a vast number of Internet sites.

Field research is about gathering information by communicating directly with people, whether through printed questionnaires, face-to-face or telephone interviews with individuals, consumer panel sessions, or online focus group sessions where the participants give their views in a chat room.

EXTENSION 1
Market research requires a number of skills that any manager may find useful from time to time. If you would like to go into the subject in more depth and learn about some of the techniques involved, you might like to read *Do Your Own Market Research* by P. N. Hague and P. Jackson.

Interpreting the results of this research has to be done with great care as it's easy to draw misleading conclusions. Once famous example of this was provided by Coca Cola in 1985, when the company decided to replace its old formula with a new sweeter, and less tangy, variation. The decision was based on taste tests that showed a distinct preference for the new formula. But the new-style Coke was instantly unpopular with the general public and the company was forced to put the old Coke back on the market after only 87 days.

This story doesn't, of course, alter the fact that it's possible for market research to reveal all sorts of customer needs that an organization may have been unaware of.

4.2 How much satisfaction should you give?

Should you not try to meet all the needs of the customer, if you can get away with it?

Customer care costs money and effort, but if your standards of performance slide, you will soon be in trouble, even if you have little competition to worry about.

Customers whose needs are not met will always go elsewhere if they can.

Should you provide exactly what customers say they need, and no more? Or should you provide them with more than this?

It usually pays to give your customers **a little more** than they expect, especially if this is in the area of human factors, which cost little or nothing. They will be impressed, and you will be more likely to keep them.

Just a little more can be enough to impress. However, sometimes you may need to give substantially more.

Activity 20 ·

In what circumstances would you have to consider giving your customers substantially more than they have expected in the past?

_____

_____

If your competitors improve their offer, you can't afford to be left behind.

Consider the motor manufacturing business. Competition is fierce and each manufacturer tries to gain a competitive edge by offering not only high discounts but also material improvements to the product, such as:

- new features;
- higher specifications;
- six-year anti-corrosion guarantees;
- free servicing for a year;
- interest-free loans;
- free membership of a motoring organization.

In other sectors, suppliers compete to win customers and keep them happy by offering:

- free trial periods (for example, office equipment suppliers);
- unconditional replacement of any item if faults appear (for example, domestic appliances);
- the opportunity to watch the work being done (for example, vehicle servicing);
- the personal attention of a customer adviser (for example, banks and building societies);
- bargain offers and special promotions;
- clubs and magazines for customers.

The danger in all this frenzied competition is that customers may come to expect more than the suppliers can afford to give them!

Activity 21

2 mins

We have clearly moved into the sphere of marketing. What would you say is the difference between customer care and marketing?

_____

_____

> Customer care is part of the marketing approach – its purpose is to retain existing customers by meeting their needs and wants.

Marketing is about identifying and satisfying the needs of the customer in a way that meets the needs of the supplier (the need being to make a profit, to grow, or to survive in a healthy condition, and so on).

The marketing approach covers everything from the design of the product to the way it is delivered. It is concerned both with winning new customers and retaining old ones.

Supermarkets' loyalty cards are an example of how marketing and customer care are interlocked. Loyalty cards are designed to give customers a financial incentive to shop with a particular chain, thus increasing market share.

They are also part of a wider marketing strategy, which generates marketing data that can help plan the mix of product lines and even the best location for new stores.

Like many marketing initiatives, loyalty cards worked well to begin with, but now all the major supermarket chains have introduced them. Loyalty cards no longer confer a marketing advantage: customers now expect them as a matter of course, and may hold cards for several different store chains.

Activity 22

15 mins

S/NVQ
F6

This Activity may provide the basis of appropriate evidence for your S/NVQ portfolio. If you are intending to take this course of action, it might be better to write your answers on separate sheets of paper.

1   Who is your own most important customer? (This may be an internal or external customer.)

_____

2 What are this customer's needs in relation to you and your team?

_____

_____

_____

3 How well do you meet these needs under the main customer satisfaction headings (ring the statement which is nearest the truth)?

	very well	quite well	so-so	not very well	very badly
a product factors?	1	2	3	4	5
b convenience factors?	1	2	3	4	5
c human factors?	1	2	3	4	5

Think carefully about your answers:

■ customers' needs may be greater than you think they are;

■ you may not be meeting these needs as well as you think you are.

4 In what specific areas, if any, do you think improvements should be made?

_____

_____

_____

5 Consult with your line manager and at least one other colleague. Do they have any further ideas on where improvements could be made?

_____

_____

_____

In case anyone in your team still feels that internal customers aren't really important, remind them that:

■ your organization depends on how well it serves its external customers;
■ if you aren't serving them, you are certainly serving the people who are!

5 The quality of personal service

A Director of a large retail chain paid a surprise visit to a rather run-down store in her group, where no one knew her. She found a young man filling shelves and asked him her standard question to test how well staff knew their product range: 'Excuse me, where can I find black peppercorns?'

The youth's job was simply to fill shelves according to a printed schedule. But seeing a person he assumed was a customer, he replied promptly and cheerfully: 'I haven't got a clue, love, but come with me and I'll help you look for them!'

It should be obvious what customers expect from their suppliers' staff: we are all customers ourselves, and we know what good service and bad service means.

5.1 The ABC of service

The quality of customer service depends entirely on human factors. These can be summed up in the ABC of customer service:

A ttitude
B ehaviour
C ompetence.

Activity 23 · 5 mins

Think of **two** recent situations where you, as a customer, received **good** service, and another **two** where you received **poor** or **bad** service. Describe briefly what happened in each case.

Good service:

1 _____

_____

2 _____

_____

Bad service:

1 _____

_____

2 _____

_____

Here are three examples from my personal experience:

1 **Good service**

I had to hire a car, but wasn't able to collect it during the hirer's normal working hours. 'No problem sir', said the manager, 'I'll bring it out to you myself.' This involved good **attitude** (being willing to do that little bit extra to help) and good **behaviour** (being friendly and polite).

2 **Bad service**

I wanted to buy a particular technical book. I went to the desk to ask a sales assistant, but she seemed to be very busy doing something else, and didn't even look at me. After a few moments I said 'Excuse me . . .,' but, still without looking up, she said, 'Sorry, I'm busy. You'll have to ask someone else.' This involved bad **attitude** (not being willing to help) and bad **behaviour** (an unfriendly manner and failure to make eye contact).

3 **Good service**

I phoned my computer suppliers to ask about a problem I was having with a disk drive. The person who answered my call said, 'I'm sorry, sir, I'm not familiar with that particular machine, and the person who deals with them is tied up at the moment. If you'll give me your name and phone number, I'll explain what the problem is and ask her to get back to you as soon as she's free.' Half an hour later, the other person called back and sorted out my problem. That was an example of all three elements of the ABC at work: good attitude, good behaviour and **competence** (both from the person who competently passed on my message and the one who competently solved my problem).

5.2 Good attitude

The basis of a good attitude to customer care is accepting that:

- customers are the most important people in our working life;
- satisfying their needs is our most important task.

We need to respect our customers, which means meeting their needs in a way which is friendly without becoming too familiar. Managers, supervisors and team leaders should constantly remind their staff of these ideas, and make sure they provide a consistent example for the team members to follow.

■ **When team members accept that customers are the most important people**

   it makes sense to do that little bit extra to help them.

■ **When team members accept that satisfying customers' needs is the most important task**

   it makes sense to give serving customers priority over all their other tasks.

Activity 24

S/NVQ F6

This Activity may provide the basis of appropriate evidence for your S/NVQ portfolio. If you are intending to take this course of action, it might be better to write your answers on separate sheets of paper.

If you are compiling an S/NVQ portfolio, you may wish to take this Activity further by drawing up more detailed proposals for improvement, implementing them and evaluating the result.

Assess the quality of service your organization provides and identify any problems in relation to caring for your customers. Make a note of them here, and outline briefly what action you can take to correct them. (You have been given room to list **five**; if there are more than this, continue on separate sheets of paper.)

Problems: **Action:**

1   _____   _____

    _____   _____

    _____   _____

2   _____   _____

    _____   _____

    _____   _____

3 _____   _____

   _____   _____

   _____   _____

4 _____   _____

   _____   _____

   _____   _____

5 _____   _____

   _____   _____

   _____   _____

Attitude problems among your team members are basically a management issue, and usually come down to the sort of example that you and other managers give, and the quality of the leadership that you provide.

5.3 Behaviour

Behaviour means what you actually do for (and to) the customer. Staff may have a very good attitude towards customers without knowing how to put this into practice.

Anyone who deals with customers must treat them the way they expect to be treated – which is promptly, efficiently and with respect. In general, customers do **not** like staff who are:

■ scruffily dressed, badly groomed, or sloppy in their behaviour;
■ inattentive, off-hand, rude, sarcastic or superior;
■ lazy, slow, careless or uncommunicative.

Personal standards are important: it is difficult to show respect for the customer if you cannot demonstrate self-respect first! At the point of contact with the customer, this becomes very important. First impressions count!

Activity 25 · 4 mins

Your organization probably has a 'front-person' of some kind (a receptionist, a secretary, or perhaps a security guard) who is the first point of contact with customers and other visitors arriving at your premises. Think about a new customer on coming face to face with this front-person for the first time. What would that customer expect him or her to do? List the first **three** things that should happen:

1 _____

2 _____

3 _____

The customer will expect a suitable greeting, and in particular:

1 to be given immediate attention;

2 to be given friendly signs (which should include a smile and eye contact);

3 to be greeted with friendly but polite words (such as 'good morning, how can I help you?').

This is quite different from the reception I had from the bookshop assistant in my earlier example. She made two basic errors:

■ she failed to give me her attention;
■ she failed to make eye contact.

In fact the signs she gave me were very unfriendly.

Activity 26 · 6 mins

Non-verbal communication, or body language – the signals we send each other by the way we behave – is much more important than most people realize.

Imagine entering an unfamiliar office for the first time, and coming up to the reception desk. How would you interpret the following examples of body language on the part of the receptionist?

1   The receptionist is on the telephone, and just waves vaguely at you and carries on the phone conversation.

_____

2   The receptionist, who is busy typing at the back of the reception area, says 'Good morning, how can I help you?' but doesn't stop typing.

_____

3   The receptionist greets you politely, without a flicker of a smile.

_____

4   The receptionist greets you politely, but doesn't look you in the eye.

_____

5   When you arrive, the man at the reception desk is lounging in his chair with his feet up, smoking a cigarette. However, he greets you in a polite and friendly manner.

_____

None of these is satisfactory because in each case the receptionist is sending you **negative signals**:

■   the first one is telling you that the person on the phone is more important than you are;
■   the second is telling you that the typing he or she is doing is more important than you are;
■   the third, by not looking at you, is showing signs which to most of us suggest uneasiness, guilty feelings, or even dishonesty; when you look someone in the eye in a friendly manner, you are saying:

   ■   I'm being open and straightforward with you;
   ■   I am paying you attention.

■   the fourth, by not smiling, is showing signs of hostility; the smile is a very important human signal which says:

   ■   'don't worry, I am friendly'; and
   ■   'I really **am** glad to see you'.

■   the fifth receptionist is revealing a sloppy attitude to his work, even if the greeting he delivers is in itself satisfactory.

Meeting and greeting:

1 Show the other person you have noticed them.
2 Make eye contact.
3 Smile.
4 Greet them politely.

What could be simpler?

You probably do not have responsibility for the reception area, but the lessons should be clear:

everyone who MEETS the customer must GREET the customer.

> What we DO is as important as what we SAY.

6 Telephone contacts

Today there are many businesses whose contact with their customers is entirely through the Internet. If you want to order a book from Amazon, for example, you never speak to anyone and go through the entire process on-line. This, however, doesn't alter the fact that a very high proportion of direct customer contacts still come via the telephone. Customers may phone:

- to make an inquiry;
- to place an order;
- to make an appointment;
- to chase a job;
- to complain.

Some organizations, like the gas, electricity, water and telephone companies, have entire departments whose only job is to provide customers with information, but there are many organizations where almost anyone can find themselves at the end of a phone call from an internal or external customer.

For that moment, for that customer, the person who answers the phone **is** the organization (or the department or section, if the caller is an internal customer). The reputation of the organization or department stands or falls on how well that one person copes with the customer contact situation.

Activity 27 · 2 mins

There are several big differences between customer contact on the phone and face-to-face contact, and when talking over the phone we need to bear these in mind. What would you say are the **two** most important differences?

1 _____

2 _____

Although the telephone is a very important medium of communication, the problem with it is that **less communication takes place** than when you are talking face-to-face.

■ You can't see what the people you are talking to look like.
■ You can't see the expressions on their faces.
■ You can't see what they are doing while they are talking to you.
■ You can't see what is going on around them.
■ You can't 'read' their body language to judge how they are reacting to you.

This means we have to compensate by working a little bit harder when speaking on the phone than we do in face-to-face situations.

Activity 28 · 2 mins

Suppose you have to phone another organization to ask about an order that has not materialized. The phone rings and someone picks it up. What do you think that person should say?

_____

_____

_____

Because you can't see what is happening at the other end, you don't know for certain that you've got the right number, or who is answering. Also, telephone lines distort voices, and you can't always recognize the speaker even when you know them quite well.

How not to answer
the telephone:

'Goodmorning
GambleandFidget
TravelAgentshere
HitchinBranchour
aimistoensureyour
holidayreallytakes
offthisisYiorgoshere
howcanIhelpyou.'

Most organizations believe that the person who answers should start with a polite greeting ('Good morning' or 'good afternoon' is quite enough), and then concentrate on providing sensible information.

■   State the name of the organization or department that you have reached.
■   Give his or her name.
■   Ask in a polite and friendly way how he or she can help you.

Is that the kind of quality of service your team members provide when they answer the phone? Or do they just say 'Hello' and let the other person guess who they've got through to?

6.1   Taking the necessary action

The other big issues when answering the telephone are:

■   whether you are able to deal with the call yourself;
■   what you do if you can't deal with the call yourself.

Activity 29

8 mins

Try to suggest some simple rules for how your staff should behave in these circumstances:

1   The person who takes the call can answer the enquiry, though it isn't really his or her job to do so.

_____

_____

2   The person who takes the call can answer the enquiry but feels too busy to do so at that particular moment.

_____

_____

44

3   The person who takes the call cannot answer the enquiry, but can transfer the caller to someone who can.

_____

_____

4   The person who takes the call cannot answer the enquiry, and the person who can is not available.

_____

_____

Here are some suggestions, based on accepted 'good practice':

1   **Can answer, but it isn't his or her job.**

Unless there is a very strong reason for not answering, this person should take the responsibility for doing so and make the extra effort to satisfy the customer's needs.

2   **Can answer, but too busy.**

The customer's needs should come first, so there would have to be a very strong reason for not answering there and then; if there is, this person should:

1 apologize;
2 take the customer's name and number;
3 arrange to phone back within a stated time;
4 keep to this promise.

3   **Cannot answer, but can transfer to someone who can.**

Customers generally hate being transferred; if someone has to do so, they should:

1 tell the customer what they are doing;
2 explain to whom they are transferring them;
3 give that person the customer's name and details of the enquiry before making the transfer.

4   **Cannot answer, and the person who can isn't there.**

This is the source of many grumbles from customers, because in this situation the customer is often asked to phone again without any guarantee of success, and messages taken often get lost; the person taking the call should:

1 tell the customer the name of the person who can answer them;
2 promise to make sure that they will do so;

> Many large organizations such as utilities operate a 'one-stop shop' for inquiries. Staff are trained to deal with 80 per cent or more of customer's queries on the first call, though only after the customer has listened to a recorded message telling them which numbers on their phone to press regarding particular types of enquiry.

3 take down the customer's name, number and other details;
4 take responsibility for ensuring that the named person keeps this promise.

Simple enough, but we all have experience of people who:

■ can't see why information is such an important part of customer service;
■ won't take responsibility for doing that little extra bit of service that keeps a customer happy;
■ don't keep the service promises that they make.

6.2 Competence

So far in this session we have looked at two components of the ABC of customer service: attitude and behaviour. The final component is competence, that is being able to give the answers and provide the service that customers require.

Customers will accept being efficiently transferred to a competent person, or being told that a competent person will phone them back. But it would be much better if the person who spoke to them in the first instance was able to provide a proper answer.

Of course, this isn't always possible, but managers should try to ensure:

■ that phone calls are fielded by people who can competently answer them;
■ that members of the team are given the training and experience that will equip them to answer competently as soon as possible.

Failure to provide proper service on the phone is just one of many things that contribute to poor customer care, and which can easily result in a complaint.

Self-assessment 2 ·

10 mins

I   Complete the following sentence so that it makes sense:

Customer care is about serving customers in a way that meets their

_____ and _____.

2   Comment briefly on these statements:

a If your organization loses customers it can always replace them.

_____

_____

b Customer care is mainly about the quality of the customer contact staff.

_____

_____

c The product factors are the most important element in customer satisfaction.

_____

_____

d Caring for customers and marketing are separate issues.

_____

_____

3   On a typical day, Mullet and Hake Ltd upset three customers but please seven. Will their reputation be rising or falling, and why?

_____

4   Unscramble the words in brackets to show what customers want above all from the services supplied to them:

a complete (IRA BITE LILY) _____ and

b no (RUSS'S PIER) _____

5   Why is it good policy to give customers a little more than their stated needs?

_____

_____

_____

_____

6   Complete these **two** sentences so that they make sense.

a Customers' _____ may be greater than you _____ .

b You may not be _____ these as well as you think you are.

7   Unscramble the words in brackets so that these statements make sense:

a (MAIN TIN ROOF) _____ is a very important part of customer service.

b Always make sure that your service (RIPE MOSS) _____ are kept.

8   What is the ABC of personal service?

A _____   B _____   C _____

9   Complete these sentences by adding the missing half:

a When team members accept that customers are the most important people, then _____

b When team members accept that satisfying customers' needs is the most important task, then _____

c It is difficult to show respect for the customer if _____

10   What messages are sent by these examples of body language?

a Avoiding eye contact.

_____

b Smiling.

_____

c Putting aside the work you are doing and approaching the customer.

_____

Answers to these questions can be found on pages 131–2.

7 Summary

- Customer care is part of marketing. Its aim is to keep existing customers happy by serving them in a way that meets their needs and wants.

- It is ten times easier and ten times cheaper to keep an existing customer satisfied than to win a new one.

- Every aspect of the service you provide plays a part in customer satisfaction under one of these headings:

    - product factors (the right product at the right price);
    - convenience factors (at the right place and right time);
    - human factors (in the right way).

- Dissatisfied customers do not always complain, but they will tell other people and will take their business elsewhere if they can.

- It is important to listen for dissatisfaction and to deal with the problem early by:

    - monitoring complaints;
    - asking customers' opinions.

- The aim should be to provide a service that is more than customers expect.

- It is the service as a whole that creates customer satisfaction, and everyone in an organization contributes to that service in some way.

- If you're not serving external customers yourself, make sure you provide the right service for the people who do.

- Most employees have at least some direct contact with customers, and should be trained in how to behave in a way that will please the customer.

- The quality of personal service depends on the ABC:

    A ttitude
    B ehaviour
    C ompetence.

- The basis of a good attitude is accepting that:

    - customers are the most important people in our working life;
    - satisfying their needs is our most important task.

- The basis of good behaviour when in direct contact with the customer is to treat him or her with respect, in particular:

  - being smart and well-groomed (signs of self-respect);
  - giving them your immediate attention;
  - giving them friendly signs (including a smile and eye contact);
  - greeting them with friendly but polite words.

- Everyone who meets the customer must greet the customer.

- What we do is as important as what we say.

- When the contact is by telephone we need to make extra efforts:

  - stating clearly who and what you are;
  - taking accurate messages;
  - keeping customers clearly informed of what you are doing (e.g. when transferring them to someone else).

- Keeping promises is a vital part of customer care.

Session C
Delivering customer care

1 Introduction

It is impossible to deliver customer care successfully unless everyone in the organization is committed to doing so. There will be a failure to deliver:

- if Sales are committed, but Despatch are not;
- if Reception are committed but Administration are not;
- if Production are committed but Stores are not.

In this session we look at how to achieve a commitment to delivering total customer satisfaction. This will involve you in:

- checking how satisfied your customers currently are;
- identifying the problem areas;
- identifying the root causes;
- finding ways of overcoming them.

2 Identifying your customer care problems

Do you have a problem? Yes.

We can say this with confidence because:

- not even the most popular organizations get it right every time for every customer;
- customers' needs and expectations are always changing.

What is good enough today will not be good enough tomorrow. The most successful organizations believe in acting **now** to make sure they meet tomorrow's needs.

Absolute perfection is not attainable. Your target for customer care should be **continuous improvement towards perfection.**

The first step is to identify any shortcomings.

2.1 Asking the customer

Carisbrooke Cleaning Services provided contract office cleaning for numerous local firms. They were very competitive on price, and very responsive to their customers' complaints. Their policy was that whenever a customer complained, a supervisor and a back-up cleaner would arrive within two hours to check the problem and put it right. (Cleaning normally took place out of office hours.)

Many customers were impressed with the efficiency of this service but, as time went on, they became less impressed. Several customers began to ask CCS why their night cleaners couldn't do the job properly in the first place, and thus avoid the disruption involved in putting problems right during the day.

You may **think** you are providing an excellent service, but only your customers can tell you for certain. Many organizations now work quite hard to find out what their customers think of them. Here is a part of a questionnaire issued by a Health Authority to try to find out how well the needs of outpatients using a huge hospital are being met.

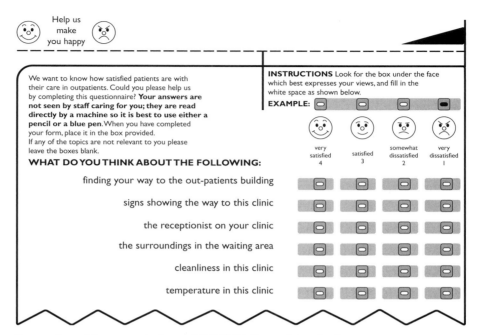

Reproduced by permission of CASPE Consulting Ltd.

A big hospital deals with very large numbers of patients, so this form is designed to be scored automatically using a computer, but this would not be necessary for smaller organizations.

Clearly, this is a serious exercise to find out what is right and what is wrong, so that action can be taken to improve the situation in the future.

Now let's put the spotlight on you, your department or section, and your team. It may not be your direct responsibility to satisfy external customers, so instead let's see how well you are satisfying the expectations of your internal customers.

Remember the ABC of customer satisfaction – Attitude, Behaviour, Competence.

Activity 30

S/NVQ
F6

1 Choose one of your main internal customers from the list you made in Activity 7 on page 12.

2 Draw up a list of up to ten questions that you could ask, in order to find out how well you are satisfying this customer (the first one has been suggested for you, but change it if you wish). Try to put yourself in your customers' shoes, and ask the questions that will be most relevant to them.

The rating scale will help you measure how satisfied your customers are. Circle your response.

How satisfied are you with:	Very	Fairly	Moder-ately	Not very	Not at all
a the speed with which we react to your requests?	5	4	3	2	1
b _____	5	4	3	2	1
c _____	5	4	3	2	1
d _____	5	4	3	2	1
e _____	5	4	3	2	1
f _____	5	4	3	2	1
g _____	5	4	3	2	1
h _____	5	4	3	2	1
i _____	5	4	3	2	1
j _____	5	4	3	2	1

Of course, everyone who does this Activity will need to ask different questions, and they will probably need to be different for each customer. You will need:

■ to identify all the important aspects of the service you supply;
■ to be specific.

Asking a very general question such as 'How satisfied are you with our service?' will probably not tell you enough.

Here is an example of how one manager approached this Activity.

The manager of the Publications Department of a local authority decided to send out the following brief questionnaire to her customers – the departments dealing directly with the public.

How satisfied are you with:	Very	Fairly	Moderately	Not very	Not at all
1 the speed with which we produce designed documents?	5	4	3	2	1
2 the quality of design of our work?	5	4	3	2	1
3 our understanding of your requirements?	5	4	3	2	1
4 the way we deal with urgent jobs?	5	4	3	2	1
5 the way we respond to queries from you on progress with individual jobs?	5	4	3	2	1
6 the way we handle corrections?	5	4	3	2	1
7 our attitude to special requests (such as unusual packaging for information packs or special paper for leaflets)?	5	4	3	2	1
8 the way we deal with you on a personal level?	5	4	3	2	1

Are there any other points about our service that you would like to make?

Please add them here:

_____

_____

Having read this, do you think that you should change any of your own questions before you try them out?

Activity 31

S/NVQ F6

This Activity may provide the basis of appropriate evidence for your S/NVQ portfolio. If you are intending to take this course of action, it might be better to write your answers on separate sheets of paper.

If you are compiling an S/NVQ portfolio you may decide to take this Activity further by:

- discussing the findings with your team;
- drawing up a list of the actions needed to put right any shortcomings;
- putting these into effect.

1   Revise your short questionnaire if necessary, and write or word process it neatly on a clean sheet of paper. Discuss it with your line manager and get his or her approval to use it. (You may need to make further changes after this discussion.)

2   Now contact your customer, explain what you are doing and why, and give them copies of the questionnaire to complete; alternatively, go through the questionnaire personally with them.

3   When the questionnaire comes back to you, review the results and if necessary discuss them with your customer to get clarification.

This could also provide appropriate evidence for your portfolio.

2.2 Looking at the results

The ratings your customers give you may be good, bad or indifferent, but in most cases they will show that **some aspects of your service are less satisfactory than others.**

Activity 32

4 mins

The Publications Department in our earlier example received the following ratings from its Customer Satisfaction Questionnaire:

How satisfied are you with:	Very	Fairly	Moder-ately	Not very	Not at all
1 the speed with which we produce designed documents?	5	4	③	2	1
2 the quality of design of our work?	5	④	3	2	1
3 our understanding of your requirements?	5	④	3	2	1
4 the way we deal with urgent jobs?	5	4	③	2	1
5 the way we respond to queries from you on progress with individual jobs?	5	4	3	②	1
6 the way we handle corrections?	5	④	3	2	1
7 our attitude to special requests (such as unusual packaging for information packs or special paper for leaflets)?	5	④	3	2	1
8 the way we deal with you on a personal level?	5	4	3	②	1

Try to sum up what this questionnaire tells us, in a couple of sentences.

_____

_____

_____

_____

_____

_____

As you saw in Session B, customer satisfaction factors fall into three groups:

- product-related factors (the right product at the right price);
- convenience factors (at the right place at the right time);
- human factors (in the right way).

Total customer satisfaction comes when all these factors are right.

The Publications Department's customers are quite satisfied with the product-related factors: quality of the work (2), understanding of requirements (3), the response to special requests (7) and handling of corrections (4). They are less happy with the convenience factors: general speed (1) and dealing with urgent jobs (3). They are particularly unhappy with the human factors: the response to queries on progress (2) and personal contacts in general (8).

It is clear that the Publications Department has problems with turning work round fast enough. In order to satisfy its customers, the department must start working to tighter schedules. The department may be understaffed, but just as likely is that there is a problem with organization. The manager probably needs to look at the processes involved in producing a publication and identify ways of making them more efficient. There is also a major problem with the way the department's staff communicate with people from other departments. They seem to resent being asked questions about how jobs are progressing and are generally unwilling to engage in discussion of their work, although their customers would very much like to have more input than they do at present, particularly in the initial stages of a job.

2.3 Customers' rights

All customers have legal rights, based on the contract between suppliers and customers, and good customer service is really only possible if you understand those rights. A contract is an agreement by the customer to buy (at an agreed price) particular goods or services, and the supplier to sell them. A contract doesn't need to be written down, unless it involves the sale of land or buildings, because the agreement by the buyer to give some consideration (pay money or supply other goods or services) in exchange for something creates a verbal contract. If the supplier meets the terms of the contract, then the contract is legally binding on the buyer. That means, if the seller supplies the goods asked for by the customer, then the customer must pay for them.

Making something available at a particular price doesn't mean that the supplier has to sell the product to anybody who offers to buy it, it is simply an *offer to treat*. In other words, the supplier is saying that they would be prepared to sell at that price. Only when an offer is made by a customer and accepted by a supplier is a contract formed.

Buying goods

Most contracts to buy goods (but not property) are covered by The Sale of Goods Act 1979 (and amendments to it in 1994 and 1995) and the Supply of Goods and Services Act 1982. The Sale of Goods Acts say that sellers must own the goods that they are selling, which seems like common sense. The Acts also distinguish between *expressed* and *implied terms* or conditions. Expressed terms are particular agreements entered into as part of the contract. For example, an order may say 'Supply the goods by Friday at the latest'. That is an expressed term of the contract. Goods delivered on Saturday need not be accepted or paid for by the customer, as the terms of the contract have not been met.

All contracts also have some implied terms. That means that when people agree to buy and sell something, they both imply certain conditions. Three implied terms are laid down in the Acts. Firstly, buyers have a right to expect that goods are of *satisfactory quality*. This applies to both new and second-hand goods bought from a trader, but not goods bought from a private individual. Satisfactory quality means that goods should be durable (that means that they will last a reasonable length of time in normal use), safe and have acceptable appearance. Of course, this is in relation to the price and the circumstances in which they were bought. What a customer can expect from a charity shop isn't the same as from an exclusive dress designer.

Secondly, the goods must be *accurately described* – a 'one gigabyte MP3' player can't have only 512 megabytes of memory. Thirdly, goods must be of *merchantable quality*, or fit for the purpose. This means that goods must be suitable for the use they are being put to. If a customer asks for a cartridge for a particular laser printer then the cartridge supplied must work in that printer.

A trader can't exclude any of these contract rights for consumers. The Unfair Contract Terms Act 1977 (and the Unfair Terms in Consumer Contracts Regulations 1994) say that the three basic rights (satisfactory quality, accurate description and fitness for the purpose) can't be left out or restricted for an ordinary consumer. However, a customer's Sale of Goods rights can be excluded if the goods were bought for use in a business because businesses are thought to be able to protect their own interests better than ordinary consumers.

In general, customers can return faulty goods within a reasonable period of time and demand their money back. Customers do not have to accept replacement goods, free repairs or credit notes if the goods don't meet the terms of the contract, implied or expressed. However, suppliers can refuse to give a refund if the goods have had some reasonable use and they can offer only to repair or replace them or to give a credit note. The time limit will vary with the goods and the amount of use. A £10 pair of trainers can't be expected to last as long as a £100 pair of hiking boots, even though the boots may get harder wear. All rights to compensation are lost in any case after a maximum of six years (five years in Scotland).

When goods are bought from a retailer or a distributor, the contract is always with them, not the manufacturer. However, the manufacturer may offer a guarantee. This adds to the customers rights, it doesn't replace them. Generally speaking, guarantees add to the time within which faults in the goods can be put right. Extended warranties sold by retailers do the same. Neither replaces the customers' rights under the Sale of Goods Acts.

Buying services

There are also three implied terms in contracts for services, set by The Supply of Goods and Services Act 1982. These are that *reasonable care and skill* must be taken when supplying a service, that the service must be completed in a *reasonable time* and that it must be completed at a *reasonable charge*, if a price wasn't agreed in advance Reasonable care means that the supplier takes care to avoid any obvious risks. If the supplier is a specialist, then they are more likely to be aware of the possible problems which someone else wouldn't know about.

If a job is done badly, a customer has the right to demand that the supplier puts them right or completes the job or they can get someone else to do it and take legal action to recover the extra cost. Reasonable time means that suppliers can't disappear halfway through their work and not return for weeks. They would be failing in an implied term of the contract, even if no completion date was agreed. And the price can't be exorbitant. If there are any special reasons for abnormally high prices, like having to finish a job by working long hours, then the customer must be warned.

Many organisations supply only goods or only services, but some supply a combination of goods and services, such as installing equipment they supply. Knowing what their rights are helps you to ensure that these are met at the very least, but many organisations offer more than the minimum level of customer service required by law. However, if these additional rights are promised at the time of the sale, they become part of the expressed conditions of the contract, and the customers are legally entitled to these rights.

Activity 33

A customer has asked a local computer store for a computer to be supplied and set up in her home with a broadband service, to enable her to develop her hobby of tracing her family's history. The shop assistant suggests that she buy a particular PC that has a very high specification and promises to get the broadband service organised for installation by the end of the following week.

In fact, the installation doesn't take place until three weeks later and the broadband connection takes a further two weeks to be set up. When the customer's friend visits she asks why she bought such a highly specified machine as it was far more powerful than she needed, and a machine for half the price would have been perfectly suitable.

The customer complains to the shop manager, who apologises for the delay but says that they have fulfilled their contract as the system is working OK and that she should have chosen a less expensive machine when she placed her order. He denies any responsibility for her having a more powerful machine that she required.

Is the shop manager right? What rights, in law, does the customer have?

_____

_____

_____

_____

_____

_____

The answer to this Activity can be found on page 98.

2.4 Customer complaints

Every organization receives its share of complaints, and these days it could even be said that a complaints industry exists. Some organizations have their own complaints departments, while others, including the gas, electricity, telephone and water utilities, are watched over by statutory authorities – such as Ofgas, Oftel, and Ofwat – whose job is to monitor complaints and urge action.

These bodies may have the power to inflict financial penalties if complaint levels get out of hand, or if complaints are dealt with too slowly.

2.5 Dealing with complaints

The most sensible approach to complaints is to prevent them, by providing the right products at the right place and time, and in the right way. But it is hard to eliminate them altogether.

Activity 34

2 mins

When a customer (internal or external) complains, what is your work team's usual reaction? Tick the answer which best describes their usual behaviour and attitude.

1   They try if possible to ignore it, cover it up, or shuffle the   ❐
     problem off onto someone else.

2   They become defensive, make excuses and even argue   ❐
     with the customer.

3   They try to buy the customer off with compensation of some kind.   ❐

4   They listen carefully and try to deal with the problem promptly and   ❐
     efficiently.

5   They regard the complaint positively as an opportunity to   ❐
     strengthen links with the complaining customer.

Here are some comments on these five positions:

1   **They try if possible to ignore it, cover it up, or shuffle the problem off onto someone else.**

This is a very poor approach which does nothing to solve the customer's problem, and indeed may even make it worse, resulting in further complaints and more work.

2   **They become defensive, make excuses and even argue with the customer.**

Although this reaction may seem natural, it is ineffective; the customer is not interested in excuses and arguing will only serve to irritate the customer further.

3   They try to buy the customer off with compensation of some kind.

Staff who are embarrassed or frightened by a customer's complaint often try to offer compensation in the form of a rebate, a gift, or some extra service; this is not generally a good idea, because, although the customer may accept it, it does nothing to put right the fundamental problem.

4   They listen carefully and try to deal with the problem promptly and efficiently.

This is good, in fact a sympathetic hearing is the first thing a customer wants; it should be followed up with efficient handling of the problem.

5   They regard the complaint positively as an opportunity to strengthen links with the complaining customer.

This may sound odd: aren't complaints by their very nature negative? Perhaps, but research has shown that they are also an opportunity. This is because, in British society, at least, most people do not like to complain directly. They are much more likely to say nothing and 'vote with their feet' by using another supplier next time.

> Complaints are an important source of management information.

Many large organizations now take the view that customers who complain are valuable assets who are worth cherishing:

- they tell us about faults in our product or service of which we may not have been aware;
- property treated, they become better and more loyal customers than those who do not complain.

Customers seem to prefer a supplier who can recognize a problem and put it right efficiently to one who is always 'perfect'. After all, no one is perfect for ever, and you never know what will happen on the inevitable day when the perfection fails . . .

2.6 Anger and apologies

Finally, there are those customers who not only have a complaint, but are angry about it.

This may seem the most difficult kind of problem to deal with, but really the answer is quite simple:

deal with the problem, and the anger will subside.

The rules for dealing with angry customers are these:

DO
- listen;
- be sympathetic;
- concentrate on providing a solution to the problem;

DON'T
- offer excuses;
- argue;
- waste time trying to placate the customer's anger.

If you deal with the problem, the anger will soon go away. And remember, customers aren't always right, but you should treat them as if they are!

Activity 35   5 mins

No organization likes receiving complaints, but a number of leading companies now take the view that complaints can be positively beneficial in increasing customer loyalty. Try to suggest why this might be.

_____

_____

_____

_____

The logic goes like this.

- Some customers do not complain, they simply 'vote with their feet', i.e. they stop using the organization and go to a competitor next time.
- The long-term attitude of those who do complain depends on how well an organization deals with the complaint; customers whose problem is promptly, efficiently and pleasantly resolved are likely to have a **higher opinion** of the organization than they did before the problem arose; they become more loyal, not less.
- Complaints are an important source of feedback about how well a product is performing; if you listen carefully and take the necessary measures, you can improve your product in the future.

2.7 Looking for the causes

You have to identify the causes to solve the immediate problem and to improve service in the longer term.

Activity 36

2 mins

The Publications Department staff are seen as unco-operative and uncommunicative. What would you suggest is the root cause of these shortcomings? Tick any of these which you think may explain why these people behave the way they do:

The customers' demands are unreasonable. ☐

The Publications staff are naturally unfriendly and unhelpful. ☐

The Publications staff need more skill training. ☐

The Publications staff are unaware of what is required of them in terms of customer care. ☐

Managers and team leaders are setting a poor example. ☐

The company's policy in general is faulty. ☐

Let us discuss these in turn.

■ **The customers' demands are unreasonable**

Certainly not. The whole point of customer care is to satisfy the demands of customers as fully as possible. Customers are **not** always right, but they have to be treated as if they were!

■ **The Publications staff are naturally unfriendly and unhelpful**

Highly unlikely. Most people are naturally friendly and helpful, and there is no reason why this group of people should be any different.

■ **The Publications staff need more skill training**

No. The problem is not one of skills, for which they received good customer satisfaction ratings.

■ **The Publications staff are unaware of what is required of them in terms of customer care**

Quite probably. None of us performs properly when we don't know what standards are expected of us. The standards themselves may be quite simple, such as 'always answer the telephone within four rings', but they have to be set by management. This seems to be a problem in this particular case.

■ **Managers and team leaders are setting a poor example**

True. Here is what the department supervisor had to say on the subject:

> 'We concentrate on doing the job we're told to do. We have high standards and we're pretty efficient. But we can't have people endlessly pestering us for information or trying to have their say on the design. That would just disrupt things and make our job more difficult.'

If managers see customers as nuisances who make doing the job more difficult, then how can the staff be expected to treat them any differently?

> If supervisors don't see the need to make that extra effort, why should the staff?

■ **The company's policy in general is faulty**

This may well be true. Many organizations still do not understand the importance of total customer satisfaction, or of the need to treat other departments as internal customers.

The problem with the Publications Department starts much higher in the organization as shown below.

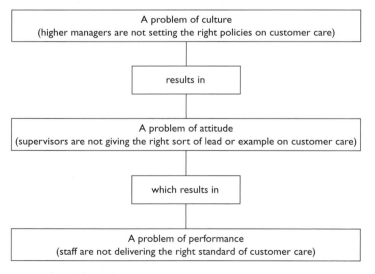

An organizational problem chain

Here is a different situation, where the problem lies with product quality.

> Redeye Ltd makes outdoor lamps with PIR (Passive Infra-Red) detectors, which automatically switch the lights on for five minutes when someone approaches. Most of its products are sold through large retailers or by mail-order.
>
> A newly introduced model, the Redeye P3010, is causing problems. Roughly 6 per cent of units sold are being returned to the retailers because the light fails to switch off again after the prescribed time.

Like the earlier example of Carisbrooke Cleaners, the Redeye case study points to a quality assurance problem. Redeye's retail customers will be very unhappy with a product which:

- upsets their own consumers;
- loses them sales;
- involves them in extra administrative work.

Redeye **must** clear up this quality problem if it wants to satisfy its customers and succeed commercially.

3 Managing for customer satisfaction

A useful formula for improving customer satisfaction!

3.1 A CASCADE of quality

In both production and services, one effective route to quality of service and total customer satisfaction is the CASCADE formula shown below.

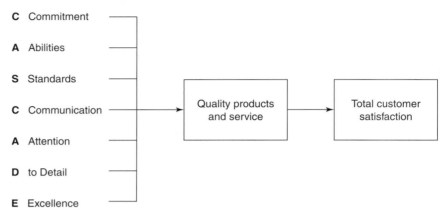

The CASCADE formula

This really comes down to quality of management: it is the manager's task to achieve a CASCADE of quality towards customer satisfaction.

EXTENSION 2
For more about the concept of excellence and how it applies to customer care, see Sarah Cook's *Customer Care Excellence*.

- **Commitment** to customer satisfaction from the work team can only come if managers and team leaders demonstrate clearly their own commitment to it.
- **Ability** is crucial: staff must have the skills needed to perform to standard, whether they work in production, in a service capacity, or in direct customer contact roles.
- **Standards** must be set and monitored, so that everyone knows what the target is and what more needs to be done to achieve it.
- Lack of proper **communication** between managers, team leaders and staff leads to misunderstandings, errors and dissatisfaction. No one can produce a quality product in these conditions.
- **Attention** to **detail** marks the difference between those who only talk about customer satisfaction, and those who are really committed to succeed.
- **Excellence** is the result, if the formula is followed.

3.2 Commitment

The Board of Directors of Hoplite Engineering Contracts Ltd decided that better customer care was the answer to an increasingly difficult competitive situation. They told the Managing Director to deal with the matter, and the MD told the Personnel Manager to devise a customer care training programme for the staff. The Personnel Manager drew up some rules for customer care, and issued them to all departmental managers, with the instruction to 'Bring these new rules to the attention of your staff'. Later, she brought in a lecturer from a local college to give groups of staff short talks on the subject.

Activity 37 · 6 mins

The programme achieved very little. Why do you think this was?

_____

_____

> **Managers must demonstrate a clear personal commitment to customer care: if they don't set the right example, they can't expect the workforce to follow.**

Any manager who thinks that customer care programmes are just a matter 'for the lower orders' is making a serious error. Customer care is a cultural issue, and it requires the whole organization to review its attitudes. In order to work, a customer care programme:

- must start at the top;
- must involve everyone;
- must have complete commitment from all levels of management.

3.3 Ability (competence)

No one starts life with the in-built ability to deliver customer satisfaction. We all have to learn the necessary skills, such as:

- the skill to machine a component to the right tolerances;
- the skill to clean an office to the right standard;
- the skill to prepare a report within the required time;
- the skill to handle a customer's complaint in the required manner.

Experience tells us that people who are fully competent in their work are more likely to be proud of what they do, and more likely to deliver a quality service.

This leads us to the conclusion that **quality customer care depends on ability and training.**

Activity 38

5 mins

What steps might you take to improve your own and your team's ability to deliver a better quality of service? Try to suggest at least **two** steps.

_____

_____

You might consider:

■ getting yourself better trained, including perhaps learning to be a more effective trainer;
■ negotiating with your own manager or with your organization's training department to provide more training resources for your team;
■ looking for ways to expose team members more directly to customers, so that they can better understand their needs;
■ giving team members more responsibility for the quality of the products or services that they provide.

3.4 Standards and communication

In order to produce or provide a high-quality product or service that satisfies customers' needs, staff first have to know what standards they are expected to achieve. The standards then have to be monitored and areas for improvement identified. All this requires more than a little thought and planning, as you will see when we return to the subject of standards in the next section.

Ideally standards should be agreed with the members of staff who will be responsible for achieving them. This calls for communication, as does:

■ discussing the results of monitoring standards;
■ establishing what improvements need to be made;
■ discussing how improvements are to be achieved;
■ reporting back on progress in implementing improvements.

It is clear that communication has a key role to play in establishing a quality service.

Activity 39 · 3 mins

Note down **two** or **three** kinds of information that you need to communicate to your own work team about achieving high quality service and customer satisfaction in a particular job.

_____

_____

_____

As in many other aspects of work, team leaders may need to make sure that the members of their work team understand:

- what the job entails;
- who the customer is, whether internal or external;
- what the required standards of performance are;
- how the job is to be done;
- when the job is to be completed;
- why it is needed.

In fact, when you think about it, all the information about a job has to do with quality, because to satisfy the customer, the job must be done:

- correctly;
- on time;
- thoroughly.

In other words, it must be done in a way which will satisfy all the customer's expectations.

3.5 Attention to detail

Total customer satisfaction doesn't appear by chance. It requires a great deal of thought and planning, and careful control of processes and functions.

Planning at the strategic level is usually the job of senior management. Detailed planning and control of individual tasks is usually delegated to more junior managers and team leaders, and this is where attention to detail is crucial.

However high the commitment, and however good the intentions, it is attention to detail that:

- often makes one organization's products or services score over those of its competitors;
- makes the most lasting and loyal customers;
- puts the seal of quality on the work that you do.

4 Setting and monitoring standards

An important principle to bear in mind when setting standards is that you first need to establish what the needs of your customers are. Secondly, standard-setting should not be a one-off task. Rather, you should see it as part of a cycle of continuous improvement in which the meeting of standards leads to greater expectations on the part of customers, which in turn lead to higher standards being set and the quality of the product or service being improved further.

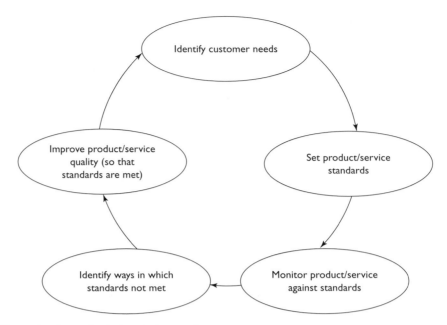

The role of standards in continuous improvement

Let's consider one simple example. You may remember that the Patient's Charter was referred to in Session A. One of the standards in the Charter was that all patients attending an outpatient clinic should be seen within 30 minutes of their appointment time. Suppose that the Ear, Nose and Throat Clinic of your local hospital succeeded in reaching this standard. To improve the quality of its service it would then have to review the standard and perhaps rewrite it as 'All patients to be seen within 20 minutes of their appointment time'.

4.1 Setting standards

It's important to word standards in a way that makes them totally unambiguous. Suppose, for example, that the manager of the local authority Publications Department, discussed in Section 2, wrote the following standard:

All queries about progress on jobs to be answered quickly.

This immediately raises the question of what is meant by 'quickly'. Does it mean within five minutes, within one hour, or even within 24 hours? The standard must be much more precise to be of any use.

Activity 40

Which of the following standards drawn up by the manager of the Publications Department would you say are ambiguous? How would you improve them?

		Ambiguous	Unambiguous
1	All requests for ideas on the basic design of documents to receive a positive response within 24 hours.	❐	❐
2	All urgent jobs to be completed according to a schedule agreed between the Publications Department and the department requesting the job.	❐	❐
3	All queries on individual jobs to be dealt with promptly and politely.	❐	❐
4	All complaints about the quality of work to be investigated within 24 hours.	❐	❐

_____

_____

_____

_____

_____

_____

_____

The first standard is ambiguous because it doesn't define what a positive response is. Does it mean just a phone call from the department to say that they are intending to get some ideas down on paper and will show them to the relevant department when they're ready? Or does it mean that they will actually have something to show within 24 hours? A better wording might be: 'Ideas on the basic design of a document to be shown to the relevant department within 24 hours of being requested'.

There is not much ambiguity in the second standard. There is, however, some ambiguity in the third because no definition of 'promptly' is included. It might be better to say that:

> 'All queries on individual jobs to be dealt with politely and within 30 minutes of being made.'

The fourth standard is also ambiguous. What does 'investigate' mean in this context? Is it just a brief chat with the designer responsible for the piece of work that is being criticized, or is it an in-depth discussion with the designer, which will lead to some conclusions being drawn about the causes of the poor quality? A better form of words might be: 'All complaints about the quality of work to be investigated, and the causes of the poor quality identified and discussed with the person making the complaint, within 24 hours'.

As well as being unambiguous, standards should also be realistic and achievable. It's no good setting standards that people have no chance of attaining with the available resources. The manager of the Publications Department, for example, should not set the standard that 'Ideas on the basic design of a document to be shown to the relevant department within 24 hours of being requested' if she does not have enough staff to make this possible. If it's inevitable that staff will fail in striving to meet a standard, they will end up being demotivated. They may also feel demotivated if they are not involved in setting the standards and instead have the standards imposed on them.

So to sum up, in setting standards you need to remember that they should be:

- based on the established needs of customers;
- unambiguous;
- achievable within the available resources;
- agreed with the staff who will have to achieve them.

4.2 Monitoring standards

There is very little point in setting standards if you are not going to have a system for monitoring them and discovering when they are not being met.

Exactly which method you use will depend on the nature of the standard. Take the standard: 'Ideas on the basic design of a document to be shown to the relevant department within 24 hours of being requested'. The best way of monitoring this is to keep a record of how long it takes to respond to each request for ideas. You can then record as a percentage the number of occasions in each week when the 24-hour deadline is met.

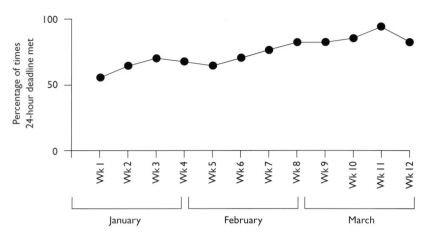

Monitoring the time taken to respond to requests for ideas

A second method is to ask customers on a regular basis – say, once a week – for their views on whether a standard is being met. Take the standard: 'All queries on individual jobs to be dealt with politely'. There is nothing here that can be measured and recorded in a graph. The alternative is to ask for customers' views on whether they feel this standard has been achieved and record their answers in a table like the one below:

	Achieved	Partially achieved	Not achieved	What needs to be done
All queries on jobs dealt with politely				

Alternatively, customers can be asked to rate the extent to which they agree/disagree with a statement relating to a standard. For example:

You are made to feel that your contributions to discussions about the design of documents are welcome.

Strongly disagree   1   2   3   4   5   Strongly agree

The mechanics of gathering the information you need to monitor standards will depend on your particular situation. You can ask staff, customers or both to complete forms and questionnaires. You can ask staff to generally monitor their own performance but also do some monitoring yourself or carry out spot checks. You can establish a group of staff as a 'quality circle' and get them to monitor standards and suggest improvements.

This brings us back to the cycle of continuous improvement that results in a quality product or service being provided. Monitoring standards will inevitably indicate areas where improvements can be made. You will need to establish what changes need to be made in work processes if standards are to be met and subsequently pushed higher.

Activity 41

15 mins

Pick out one area of work you are responsible for and try writing a standard, if possible with another member of staff, that is:

- based on the established needs of customers;
- unambiguous;
- achievable within the available resources.

_____

_____

_____

What method could you use for monitoring this standard and gathering the necessary information?

_____

_____

_____

5 A customer care culture?

To conclude this session think about the 'culture' of customer care that exists in your department or section and in the organization as a whole.

Activity 42

4 mins

EXTENSION 3
To increase customer satisfaction and loyalty, an increasing number of organizations are using what's known as Customer Relationship Management (CRM). Once a type of software, this is now a customer-centred strategy that can be adopted throughout an organization. You will find that *The CRM Pocketbook*, by Charles Turner and David Alexander, is a good book on the subject.

To find out how far you feel your group (work team, section or department), and the rest of the organization, are away from being able to provide total customer satisfaction, tick 'yes' or 'no' against the following questions.

	Within your group		Within the organization	
	Yes	No	Yes	No
■ Is the word 'customer' used frequently?	❏	❏	❏	❏
■ Is there a clear commitment to customer care on the part of managers?	❏	❏	❏	❏
■ Do people feel free to discuss the quality of customer service?	❏	❏	❏	❏
■ Are employees encouraged to bring forward their own ideas about improving quality of service?	❏	❏	❏	❏
■ Do managers and team leaders set high standards by personal example?	❏	❏	❏	❏
■ Are findings about customer satisfaction, levels of complaints, etc. made available to employees?	❏	❏	❏	❏
■ Are clear standards set for every aspect of quality and customer service?	❏	❏	❏	❏
■ When a problem arises, do the team members pool ideas to find a solution, rather than offering excuses or trying to blame one another?	❏	❏	❏	❏
■ Is the system for ensuring quality flexible and capable of dealing with new situations?	❏	❏	❏	❏
■ Is there generally a feeling of pride and achievement in the work that you do?	❏	❏	❏	❏

The more 'yes' answers you gave, the better you feel about the customer care culture in your workplace, and the more likelihood there is that total customer satisfaction is a serious issue in your working life.

If you feel that you and your team are setting higher standards in this respect than other colleagues, keep up the good work: your example can be an inspiration to others!

Self-assessment 3

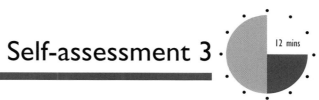

12 mins

1   Comment briefly on the following statements.

 a The only person who can reliably tell you what your customer care problems are is your line manager.

_____

_____

 b The customer is always right.

_____

_____

 c A customer care programme must start at the top.

_____

_____

 d Communication means making sure the workforce know what they have to do. It is basically a one-way process.

_____

_____

 e Customer care is all about personality.

_____

_____

2   Unscramble the words in brackets so that these statements make sense:

 a A customer care programme will not work unless it has total commitment from (TAN ME MEGAN) _____.

 b Without proper standards, no one can produce the right (FREE CORN MAP) _____.

 c It helps if team members have more (PITY BORIS'S LINE) _____ for the quality of the products or services they provide.

3 Complete the following statements.

a All consumers have certain ——————— terms in the contract to buy goods or services.

b A supplier must ensure that goods are of ——————— quality, are accurately ——————— and are ——————— for ——————— (of merchantable quality).

c A supplier must ensure services are supplied with reasonable ——————— and ———————, are completed in reasonable ——————— and at a reasonable ———————.

4 Which of the following statements are TRUE and which are FALSE?

a Standards should be set by managers on behalf of their staff. TRUE/FALSE

b Standards should always be a little higher than what is actually achievable. TRUE/FALSE

c Standards should be based on the needs of customers. TRUE/FALSE

d Standards should only be changed in exceptional circumstances. TRUE/FALSE

Answers to these questions can be found on pages 132–3.

6 Summary

- No one can afford to be complacent about the quality of customer care they provide:

    - no organization is perfect;
    - customers' needs are always changing.

- The only way to know for certain what your customers think of your service is to ask them.

- In both production and services, the CASCADE formula is an effective route to quality of service and total customer satisfaction:

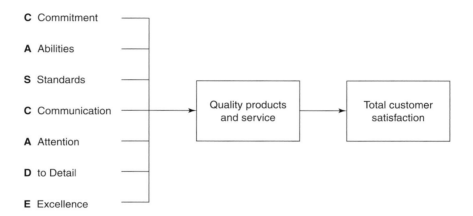

- Delivering customer care depends on the ability of higher management to establish a customer care culture:

    - it must start at the top;
    - it must involve everyone in the organization;
    - it must have complete commitment from all levels of management.

- When goods and services are bought and sold, a contract is made which has both expressed (agreed by both parties) and implied terms (set by the law). These give the customer certain rights which suppliers must satisfy.

- In order to produce or provide a high-quality product or service that satisfies customers' needs, staff first have to know what standards they are expected to achieve. The standards then have to be monitored and areas for improvement identified.

- Standards should be:

    - based on the needs of customers;
    - unambiguous;
    - achievable within the available resources;
    - agreed with the staff who have to achieve them.

- Skilful supervision and a clear example are the key to providing total customer satisfaction at the level of the work team.

Performance checks

▣ 1 Quick quiz

Jot down the answers to the following questions on Managing *Customer Service*.

Question 1   Define a customer.

_____

Question 2   Two things give customers choice. One is their spending power. What is the other?

_____

Question 3   Complete this sentence: If you aren't serving customers yourself . . .

_____

Question 4   The customers of a local authority school include the pupils and their parents. Who else?

_____

Question 5   Why is it so important to hang on to existing customers?

_____

Question 6   Complete this sentence: It is easy to get a bad reputation for service, but . . .

_____

Question 7   There are three kinds of customer satisfaction factors. Human factors and convenience factors are two of them. What is the third?

_____

Performance checks

Question 8   Which of the three kinds of satisfaction factors needs to be got right first?

_____

Question 9   What is the connection between caring for customers and marketing?

_____

Question 10   What is the ABC of personal service?

_____

Question 11   Complete this sentence: Everyone who meets the customer must . . .

_____

Question 12   Why is it so important to make eye contact when you meet a customer?

_____

Question 13   Only one person can tell you whether you are really satisfying your customers' needs. Who is it?

_____

Question 14   Where must any customer care programme start?

_____

Question 15   What above all do people need to know before they can deliver the right standards of customer care?

_____

Question 16   What is meant by 'consideration' in a contract to buy goods or services?

_____

_____

Answers to these questions can be found on pages 134–5.

2 Workbook assessment

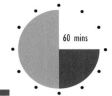

60 mins

Read the following case study and then deal with the questions which follow, writing your answers on a separate sheet of paper.

Darshana is a team leader in the payroll section of a large retail group which has 16,000 staff scattered among more than 400 local branches. Monthly pay due is calculated manually by local branch managers, and the sheets are sent to Darshana's section for processing. Her staff code the sheets and enter the details into the computer, which issues the payslips and authorizes payments.

The section is always under heavy pressure, hours are long and staff turnover is high. Darshana is authorized to bring in 'temps' whenever the work rate justifies it, but a high proportion of the staff are always fairly inexperienced, and they have a high error rate. This results in a large volume of queries and complaints: the phone is constantly ringing as staff from all over the country try to find out why their pay is wrong. Darshana allocates her most experienced staff to dealing with these queries, which take an average of 14 minutes to sort out.

Often the phone lines are permanently engaged. Everyone is harassed and frustrated, the payroll section's reputation for 'customer care' is very low, and Darshana cannot see any way out of the situation. Her boss has suggested that one way of salvaging the section's reputation would be to give the staff who handle queries special training in customer care skills, and Darshana is considering this.

Darshana's position is a very difficult one. How would you approach it? Write one or two sentences in answer to these four questions.

1   What is the basic problem here?

2   Most of the payment errors only amount to a few pounds, and are almost all corrected within a month or two. Darshana cannot really see why her customers seem to get so upset about them. Can you suggest why this is?

3   What would you say to Darshana about her boss's suggestion of special training for the staff who deal with queries?

4   What action is needed to bring this problem under control?

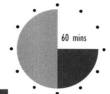

3 Work-based assignment

The time guide for this assignment gives you an approximate idea of how long it is likely to take you to write up your findings. You will find you need to spend some additional time gathering information, perhaps talking to colleagues and thinking about the assignment. The results of your efforts should be presented on separate sheets of paper.

S/NVQ
F6

Your written response to this assignment may provide the basis of appropriate evidence for your S/NVQ portfolio.

The purpose of this assignment is to make a thorough assessment of what you need to do in order to improve the quality of the care which your own department or section provides to its customers (both internal and external). You should think carefully about how you will lay out this information before beginning – it will need several columns. Previous activities should already have provided you with much of the information you need.

What you have to do

1 List all the personnel in your team, including yourself.

2 Against each one, note down the role that they play in relation to their customers. If they have direct contact, describe this briefly (for example, whether face-to-face or on the phone; how frequently; in what capacity). If they have little direct contact, describe briefly how they contribute to serving the customer (for example, by providing services for others who do).

3 Rate each person on how well they perform their responsibilities in terms of delivering a quality service to the customer. Think about their:

- attitude towards customers and service;
- behaviour in practice;
- competence to deliver the right quality of performance;

and score them on a scale of 1 (low) to 5 (high).

4 Wherever you have made a low rating, indicate what action you will take to improve it.

And don't forget to include yourself!

5 Make a list of all your customer contacts, both internal and external, with a note of the product or service (information, for example) that you supply to them.

6   Choose **five** customers from your list and write down one way in which you
    could improve the service to that customer, so that he or she gets:

- the right product;
- at the right price (if any);
- at the right place;
- at the right time;
- with the right promotion.

Reflect and review

1 Reflect and review

Now that you have completed this workbook, you should have a much clearer and more up-to-date understanding of what caring for the customer is all about, and why it is important. Focusing on a customer is not just a temporary fashion, like some ideas about management that people make a big fuss about and forget after a year or two. The more perceptive leaders of commerce and industry, like César Ritz, who said 'The customer is never wrong', have long understood that success for service industries (such as Ritz's hotels) was utterly dependent on being able to please the customer.

It's taken other organizations longer to come round to the idea, but US management experts began to take it up at over 50 years ago, and eventually it reached the rest of the world. In the last 15 years or so, 'caring for the customer' has reached non-commercial organizations too.

It is true that in the past, many organizations – particularly in manufacturing and the public sector – used to be able to soldier on without worrying too much about what their customers thought. You could have any colour as long as it was black, said Henry Ford. If they want quality, they'll be prepared to wait for it, said the manufacturers.

Firms now have to compete for customers by every means at their disposal. Customer care is one of the things that can give that crucial competitive edge.

At the same time, government has been trying to bring competitive pressure into the public sector and state services. With a customer culture growing generally, this has helped bring about a change of attitude there too.

This is the thinking behind our learning objectives for this workbook, of which the first was:

■ when you have completed this workbook you will be better able to explain the meaning and significance of customer care.

Commercial organizations are under constant pressure to outdo their rivals, and even non-commercial organizations are under ever-closer scrutiny from government and various watchdog bodies as well as from their own customers. A failure to meet customers' expectations threatens the survival of the organization and the jobs of its employees.

■ Can you explain to your team why customers are of such importance to your organization?

You must be able to convince your team of the degree to which the success of the organization and their personal futures are dependent on the customer. Why not write down the key points you would make to them?

_____

_____

_____

■ If you work in a non-commercial organization, does your team clearly understand why the people you serve should be regarded as customers?

You can find out in discussion, or perhaps with an attitude questionnaire. If you are not confident about their attitude, you should draw up a plan for changing it, using personal example, individual briefings, and perhaps group training sessions.

The second and third objectives were:

■ when you have completed this workbook you will be better able to identify your internal and external customers; and
■ you will be better able to identify your customers' needs and any areas in which you are failing to meet them.

Everyone is either serving external customers direct or serving those who are, that is, internal customers. Many are doing both. Knowing who they are – and recognizing them as customers – is the first step towards meeting their expectations.

You will also be the customer of other internal departments. Think about the service they provide, and how they could do better. Consider the service that you supply to your own internal customers in the light of this. Immersed in doing our jobs, we often assume that we are doing what our customers want when we are not. We need to listen for customer dissatisfaction – monitoring complaints, for instance – but many dissatisfied customers do not complain. The only reliable way to find out how well we are serving our customers is to ask them, for example, by using a questionnaire.

■ Have you identified your internal customers, and do you make an effort to serve them as well as an external customer might expect?
■ What do you need to do, or do differently, in order to develop a 'customer culture' in the areas for which you are responsible?

This obviously implies taking a lead and setting an example, which after all is what managers and team leaders are paid for. Hence our final two objectives:

■ when you have completed this workbook you will be better able to provide an effective lead for your team in raising the standard of customer care; and
■ you will be better able to ensure that you and your team members perform to a high standard in customer-contact situations.

Almost every aspect of customer care, from the quality of the product to the way in which it is provided, comes down to people. These people do not deliver a quality service by accident: they need to be led, supervised and trained effectively within the right overall framework.

Consider these questions and decide what further action you need to take.

■ **How well do you and your team handle face-to-face customer contacts?**

Observe your team members in contact situations and decide what improvements are needed. You may need to discuss ways of improving standards with your own manager, or your organization's training department.

■ **How well do you and your team handle contacts with customers over the telephone?**

You should listen to your team members talking on the telephone in contact situations and decide what improvements are needed. You may need to discuss how to deal with these with your own manager, or your organization's training department.

■ **How well do you and your team handle complaints from customers?**

Again, you should observe carefully how team members behave when they receive complaints. You may need to arrange training sessions as well as coaching people individually.

■ What steps can you take to improve the standards in these areas?

_____

_____

_____

_____

_____

■ How can your team make a positive contribution to strengthening the customer service 'culture' in your organization?

_____

_____

2 Action plan

Use this plan to further develop for yourself a course of action you want to take. Make a note in the left-hand column of the issues or problems you want to tackle, and then decide what you intend to do, and make a note in column 2.

The resources you need might include time, materials, information or money. You may need to negotiate for some of them, but they could be something easily acquired, like half an hour of somebody's time, or a chapter of a book. Put whatever you need in column 3. No plan means anything without a timescale, so put a realistic target completion date in column 4.

Finally, describe the outcome you want to achieve as a result of this plan, whether it is for your own benefit or advancement, or a more efficient way of doing things.

Desired outcomes			
1 Issues	2 Action	3 Resources	4 Target completion

Actual outcomes

● 3 Extensions

Extension I

Book   *Do Your Own Market Research*
Authors   P.N. Hague and P. Jackson
Edition   3rd edition, 1998
Publisher   Kogan Page

There are, of course, practical limits on what an individual can do in terms of market research, and books of this type are mainly intended for people running their own small businesses. Even so, there are plenty of practical suggestions here that someone working for a larger company could adopt to find out more about customers' needs.

Extension 2

Book   *Customer Care Excellence*
            How to Create an Effective Customer Focus
Author   Sarah Cook
Edition   4th edition, 2002
Publisher   Kogan Page

Customer Care Excellence looks at how to gain commitment from staff so that they listen to customers and develop a customer-care ethos, motivating them to deliver an excellent service at the front line, based on personal service, speed of delivery and service recovery.

Extension 3

Book   *The CRM Pocketbook*
Authors   Charles Turner and David Alexander
Edition   2001
Publisher   Management Pocketbooks

This book describes customer relationship management and explains why businesses are embracing it. It covers issues such as customer life-time values, relationship marketing, using technology and business processes in support of CRM, and the implementation of CRM in consumer and business markets.

I recommend that you take up as many of the extensions as you can. They will further increase your understanding and interest, and the extra time and effort will prove very worthwhile.

These Extensions can be taken up via your ILM Centre. They will either have them or will arrange that you have access to them. However, it may be more convenient to check out the materials with your personnel or training people at work – they may well give you access. There are other good reasons for approaching your own people; for example, they will become aware of your interest and you can involve them in your development.

4 Answers to self-assessment questions

1 Our **external** customers are the people outside the organization to whom we supply a service or product. They may be actual or **potential** customers. Our **internal** customers are the people within the organization to whom we supply something.

2 a You serve your manager, and he or she relies on the service that you provide.
   b Your manager has power over you, and it is in your interests to serve him or her well.

3 Below is one version of a customer–supplier diagram showing the internal and external relationships that exist in a prison.

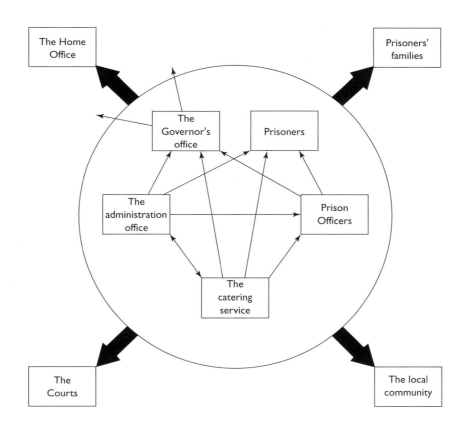

Although prisoners are there against their will, there is a strong argument for seeing them as customers, though perhaps not in quite the same way as a hotel sees its guests. Prisons are in the business of holding prisoners on behalf of the community generally, but in a way which minimizes conflict and misbehaviour. People in the local community are also customers, because the prison has to help them feel comfortable about the fact that they have large numbers of convicted criminals living very close by.

Self-assessment 2 on pages 46–8

1 Customer care is about serving customers in a way that meets their needs and wants.

2 a It is true that if your organization loses customers it can always replace them, but it is much more expensive and difficult to win new customers than to keep existing ones.

b Customer care is not mainly about the quality of the customer contact staff. Everyone in an organization contributes to the quality of the service it provides, and those who do not have direct contact with external customers should still be serving the others who do.

c The product factors are indeed the most important element in customer satisfaction. However, once the product factors are right the other factors become more significant.

d It is not correct to regard caring for customers and marketing as separate issues. Because of the impact it has on success in a competitive world, customer care must be seen as part of the marketing approach.

3 If Mullet and Hake upset three customers but please seven their reputation will on balance be falling. Dissatisfied customers tend to tell about ten other people, while satisfied ones tell only about four. The calculation here is:

	customers	people told	total	
dissatisfied	3	10	30	
satisfied	7	4		28

4 What customers want above all from the services supplied to them is:

a complete **reliability** and no **surprises**.

5 It is good policy to give customers a little more than their stated needs because they will be impressed, and you will be more likely to keep them.

6 a Customers' **needs** may be greater than you **think**.
b You may not be **meeting** these as well as you think you are.

7 a **Information** is a very important part of customer service.
b Always make sure that your service **promises** are kept.

8 The ABC of personal service is:

Attitude   **B**ehaviour   **C**ompetence

9 a When team members accept that customers are the most important people, then **it makes sense to do that little bit extra to help them**.

b When team members accept that satisfying customers' needs is the most important task, then **it makes sense to give serving customers priority over all their other tasks**.

c It is difficult to show respect for the customer if **you cannot demonstrate self-respect first**.

10 a Avoiding eye contact says you are feeling guilty, awkward or embarrassed, and that you don't want to give the other person your attention.

b Smiling says you are friendly and are glad to see the other person.

c Putting aside the work you are doing and approaching the customer shows that you consider the customer is more important than the work you were doing.

Self-assessment 3 on pages 76–7

1 a Your line manager is not the only person who can reliably tell you what your customer care problems are: your line manager may well be right, but the only person who really knows for certain is the customer.

b Customers are not always right, but you should always treat them as though they were right.

c A customer care programme must start at the top, because without a commitment from every level of management, no customer care programme can succeed.

d Communication is a two-way process: it is about listening to what the workforce have to say as well as telling them what they are required to do.

e Customer care is far from being all about personality. It is about ability, training, commitment, attitude and many other things, most of which the manager can influence.

2 a A customer care programme will not work unless it has total commitment from **management**.

b Without proper standards, no one can produce the right **performance**.

c It helps if team members have more **responsibility** for the quality of the products or services they provide.

3 a All consumers have certain IMPLIED terms in a contract to buy goods or services.

b A supplier must ensure that goods are of SATISFACTORY quality, are accurately DESCRIBED and are FIT for PURPOSE (of merchantable quality).

c A supplier must ensure services are supplied with reasonable CARE and SKILL, are completed in reasonable TIME and at a reasonable CHARGE.

4 a The statement that standards should be set by managers on behalf of their staff is FALSE. Whenever possible, standards should be agreed with the staff who will have to achieve them.

b The statement that standards should always be a little higher than what is actually achievable is FALSE. Standards should always be achievable if they are not to demotivate staff. At the same time, they should not be set so low that reaching them will do little to improve the product or service offered to customers.

c The statement that standards should be based on the needs of customers is TRUE. Customer needs, both stated and unstated, should always be the starting point for standards.

d The statement that standards should only be changed in exceptional circumstances is FALSE. Once any standard has been attained it is time to set a new higher standard in a cycle of continuous improvement.

5 Answers to activities

Activity 33 on page 00

It is doubtful if the PC supplied met the implied terms of being 'fit for purpose' since it exceeded the requirements of the user, and she could probably ask for her money back as a result – fit for purpose means that goods should be appropriate for the use that the customer has described. Being over-powerful is just as much a fault as being underpowered. Equally, there was an expressed term in the contract that the computer would be up and running by the end of three weeks. In fact it was at least one month late, so the terms of the contract had been broken. Clearly the customer had been badly served and the manager should have considered what he could do to compensate her for the bad advice and poor service.

6 Answers to the quick quiz

Answer 1   Customers are the people whom we are paid to serve, whether or not they actually buy the goods or services we produce.

Answer 2   Competition between suppliers is the other thing that gives customers choice.

Answer 3   If you aren't serving customers yourself, **you should be serving someone who is.**

Answer 4   The customers of a local authority school include pupils and their parents, but also the local authority, the community generally, the Department of Education and the government as a whole.

Answer 5   It pays to hang on to existing customers because it is so difficult and expensive to win new ones.

Answer 6   It is easy to get a bad reputation for service but **very hard to get a good one**.

Answer 7   The three kinds of customer satisfaction factors are human factors, convenience factors and product factors.

Answer 8   Of the three types of factor, product factors are the ones that must be got right first. Everything else hinges on the product.

Answer 9   Caring for customers is that part of the marketing approach which is concerned with retaining existing customers. Of course high standards and a first-class reputation for care can become marketing issues in themselves.

Answer 10   The ABC of personal service is Attitude (the way people think), Behaviour (the way people act) and Competence (their ability to deliver a quality product).

Answer 11   Everyone who meets the customer must **greet the customer**.

Answer 12   Eye contact is an absolutely crucial part of the interpersonal communication that we call body language. Not to make eye contact suggests shiftiness, embarrassment and/or lack of interest and respect.

Answer 13   Only the customer can really tell you how well you are doing in the customer care stakes.

Answer 14   Any customer care programme must start at the top.

Answer 15   The thing that people need to know above all is what standards are expected of them. Naturally, they will only meet those standards if they are properly trained, properly motivated and given the right example from above.

Answer 16   'Consideration' is the payment (or other goods and services) given in exchange for the goods or services being bought.

◼● 7 Certificate

Completion of this certificate by an authorized person shows that you have worked through all the parts of this workbook and satisfactorily completed the assessments. The certificate provides a record of what you have done that may be used for exemptions or as evidence of prior learning against other nationally certificated qualifications.

superseries

Managing Customer Service

....

has satisfactorily completed this workbook

Name of signatory ....

Position ....

Signature ....

Date ....

Official stamp

Pergamon
Flexible
Learning

Fifth Edition

superseries

FIFTH EDITION

Workbooks in the series:

Achieving Objectives Through Time Management	978-0-08-046415-2
Building the Team	978-0-08-046412-1
Coaching and Training your Work Team	978-0-08-046418-3
Communicating One-to-One at Work	978-0-08-046438-1
Developing Yourself and Others	978-0-08-046414-5
Effective Meetings for Managers	978-0-08-046439-8
Giving Briefings and Making Presentations in the Workplace	978-0-08-046436-7
Influencing Others at Work	978-0-08-046435-0
Introduction to Leadership	978-0-08-046411-4
Managing Conflict in the Workplace	978-0-08-046416-9
Managing Creativity and Innovation in the Workplace	978-0-08-046441-1
Managing Customer Service	978-0-08-046419-0
Managing Health and Safety at Work	978-0-08-046426-8
Managing Performance	978-0-08-046429-9
Managing Projects	978-0-08-046425-1
Managing Stress in the Workplace	978-0-08-046417-6
Managing the Effective Use of Equipment	978-0-08-046432-9
Managing the Efficient Use of Materials	978-0-08-046431-2
Managing the Employment Relationship	978-0-08-046443-5
Marketing for Managers	978-0-08-046974-4
Motivating to Perform in the Workplace	978-0-08-046413-8
Obtaining Information for Effective Management	978-0-08-046434-3
Organizing and Delegating	978-0-08-046422-0
Planning Change in the Workplace	978-0-08-046444-2
Planning to Work Efficiently	978-0-08-046421-3
Providing Quality to Customers	978-0-08-046420-6
Recruiting, Selecting and Inducting New Staff in the Workplace	978-0-08-046442-8
Solving Problems and Making Decisions	978-0-08-046423-7
Understanding Change in the Workplace	978-0-08-046424-4
Understanding Culture and Ethics in Organizations	978-0-08-046428-2
Understanding Organizations in their Context	978-0-08-046427-5
Understanding the Communication Process in the Workplace	978-0-08-046433-6
Understanding Workplace Information Systems	978-0-08-046440-4
Working with Costs and Budgets	978-0-08-046430-5
Writing for Business	978-0-08-046437-4

For prices and availability please telephone our order helpline
or email

+44 (0) 1865 474010
directorders@elsevier.com